Detour to Disaster

General John Bell Hood's "Slight Demonstration" at Decatur and the Unravelling of the Tennessee Campaign

Noel Carpenter

Savas Beatie

California

Library of Congress Cataloging-in-Publication Data

Names: Carpenter, Noel, author.
Title: Detour to Disaster: General John Bell Hood's "Slight Demonstration" and the Unravelling of the Tennessee Campaign / by Noel Carpenter—First Savas Beatie edition, first printing.
A Slight Demonstration: Decatur, October 1864: Clumsy Beginning of Gen. John B. Hood's Tennessee Campaign / by Noel Carpenter—First edition.
Description: El Dorado Hill, CA: Savas Beatie. pages cm. Includes bibliographical references and index.
Identifiers: ISBN 13:978-0-615-14866-3 (First Editon)
ISBN: 978-1-61121-671-4 (First Savas Beatie Edition)
eISBN: 978-1-61121-672-1
Subjects: 1. Hood, John B.—1831-1879—Military Leadership. 2. United States—History—Civil War—1864—Campaigns. 3. Decatur (Ala)—History—Civil War IV. General—Civil War—Tennessee Campaign. I. Author. II. Title.
Classification: E 467 J58 2007 / 973.737 P323p / 2007935883

First Savas Beatie Edition, First Printing

Book interior design by Carol Powell

Savas Beatie
989 Governor Drive, Suite 102
El Dorado Hills, CA 95762
916-941-6896 / sales@savasbeatie.com
www.savasbeatie.com

Savas Beatie titles are available at special discounts for bulk purchases in the United States. Contact us for more details.

Printed in the United States of America.

For Daddy, with love.

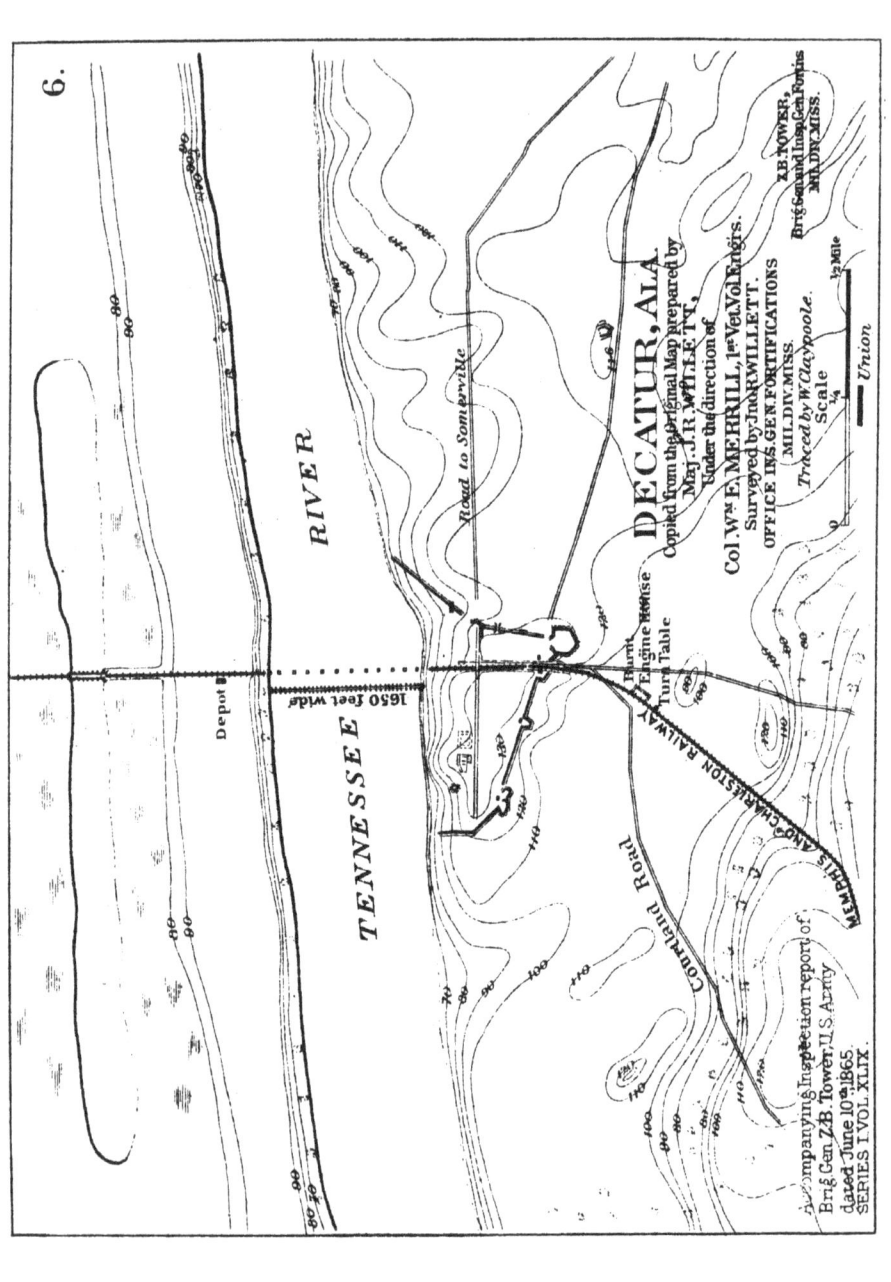

6.

DECATUR, ALA.
Copied from the original Map prepared by
Maj. J. R. WILLETT,
Under the direction of
Col. W. E. MERRILL, 1st Vet.Vol.Engrs.
Surveyed by Jno.R.WILLETT.
OFFICE INS.GEN.FORTIFICATIONS
MIL.DIV.MISS.
Traced by W.Claypoole.
Scale

Union.

Z.B.TOWER,
Brig.Gen.and Insp.Gen.Fortns.
MIL.DIV.MISS.

RIVER

TENNESSEE

Road to Somerville

Depot

1650 feet wide

Burnt
Engine House
Turn Table

MEMPHIS AND CHARLESTON RAILWAY

Copeland Road

Accompanying Inspection report of
Brig.Gen.Z.B.Tower, U.S.Army
dated June 10th 1865.
SERIES I VOL. XLIX.

CONTENTS

Foreword to the Savas Beatie Edition   vii
Foreword to the 2000 Edition   xi
Author's Preface   xii

CHAPTER ONE
Prelude — Fall of Atlanta   1

CHAPTER TWO
Hood Turns North   10

CHAPTER THREE
Tennessee Campaign Strategy   21

CHAPTER FOUR
Testing Decatur Defenses   41

CHAPTER FIVE
Vacillation, Fort Reinforced   64

CHAPTER SIX
Counterattack Stalls Demonstration   93

CHAPTER SEVEN
Counting Railroad Ties Toward Tuscumbia   121

CHAPTER EIGHT
A Reckoning   130

CHAPTER NINE
Epilogue   152

Appendix A: Organization of the Army of Tennessee   157
Appendix B: Fords and Ferries on the Tennessee River   161
Appendix C: Evacuation Order   164
Notes   165
Bibliography   178
Index   187
About the Author   202

ILLUSTRATIONS

FIGURE 1 — Gen. John B. Hood   77

FIGURE 2 — Brig. Gen. Robert S. Granger   78

FIGURE 3 — Gunboat *General Sherman*   79

FIGURE 4 — Maj. Gen. Benjamin F. Cheatham   80

FIGURE 5 — Lt. Gen. Alexander P. Stewart   81

FIGURE 6 — Maj. Gen. Samuel G. French   82

FIGURE 7 — Maj. Gen. William W. Loring   83

FIGURE 8 — Lt. Col. W.F. Prosser   84

FIGURE 9 — Col. Charles C. Doolittle   85

FIGURE 10 — Capt. Edward C. Tarrant   86

FIGURE 11 — Sgt. Joel D. Murphree   87

FIGURE 12 — Col. Thomas J. Morgan   88

FIGURE 13 — Lt. Col. Henry C. Corbin   89

FIGURE 14 — Pvt. R.H. Nations   90

FIGURE 15 — Lt. Daniel P. Smith   91

FIGURE 16 — Pontoon Bridge at Decatur   92

MAPS

Decatur, Alabama   frontis

Hood's March to Decatur and
the Tennessee Campaign   xiv

Much has been written about Confederate General John Bell Hood's tenure as commander of the Army of Tennessee from outside Atlanta in mid-July 1864 to the end of the disastrous Tennessee Campaign five months later. The Tennessee offensive ended in defeat at Franklin and Nashville, with the remnants of the army limping back to Mississippi, never again to be a major factor in the war. One might argue that too much has been written about the Tennessee Campaign. There is some fine scholarship and literature available about it. Several influential books that have shaped public opinion about the operation, however, are based upon false assumptions, bias, and the outright fabrication of events.

Strong arguments can and have been made that the overly ambitious move into Tennessee was doomed from the start. Many modern authors brush aside General Hood's postwar explanation and take an opposing view of his rationale while questioning his competence to accomplish the mission. In *John Bell Hood and the War for Southern Independence* (1982), historian Richard McMurry — by comparison with most other historians a generally sympathetic and careful Hood scholar — labeled the Tennessee Campaign an "unrealistic dream." In a later publication McMurry described it as "probably the most poorly planned and executed major campaign of the war."[1]

---

[1] Richard M. McMurry, *John Bell Hood and the War for Southern Independence* (University of Tennessee Press, 1982), 167; Richard M. McMurry, *Two Great Rebel Armies: An Essay in Confederate Military History* (University of North Carolina Press, 1989), 130-131.

In their treatment of Hood's Tennessee Campaign entitled *Five Tragic Hours: The Battle of Franklin* (1984), Thomas Connelly and James McDonough seemed to concur with McMurry, writing "[T]he difficulties and outright errors in such a plan were so profuse," they concluded, "that the scheme would have made a textbook study at West Point." Likewise, Pulitzer Prize-winning historian James McPherson depicted Hood's late 1864 plan to press into Tennessee as one that "seemed to have been scripted in never-never land."[2]

Many blame the Tennessee failure on Hood's delay in launching the invasion. The delay allowed Union General George Thomas time to consolidate, assemble, and train forces in Nashville strong enough to stop, and then nearly destroy, Hood's veteran army. William T. Sherman had provided Thomas with only John Schofield's 25,000-man veteran corps, with another 20,000-man force to be sent east to Nashville from St. Louis. This dearth of manpower compelled Thomas to train and organize Nashville quartermasters and U.S. Colored troops into infantry regiments.

Surprisingly little has been written about Hood's delay, other than it was caused by the young army commander's indecisiveness. According to Wiley Sword's *The Confederacy's Last Hurrah: The Battles of Spring Hill, Franklin, and Nashville* (1993), Hood's superiors were "livid," "frustrated," and "exasperated" at Hood's "woeful indiscretion and careless planning in the management of his army." In fact, supplies for Hood's

---

[2] James Lee McDonough and Thomas L. Connelly, *Five Tragic Hours: The Battle of Franklin* (University of Tennessee Press, 1984), 15; James M. McPherson, *Battle Cry of Freedom: The Civil War Era* (Oxford University Press, 1988), 811.

invasion were the responsibility of General Richard Taylor, in whose department the Army of Tennessee moved in preparation for the strike at Nashville.[3]

In 2007, an important but little-known monograph by amateur historian Noel Carpenter was quietly self-published by his family after Mr. Carpenter's passing. The book, originally published as *A Slight Demonstration: Decatur, October 1864: Clumsy Beginning of Gen. John B. Hood's Tennessee Campaign,* might rightly be called a micro-history. Most such books focus on minor or obscure incidents within the framework of a larger event. The minute details are often interesting, but they rarely have a major impact on the scholarship and literature of the larger event. Such is not the case with Carpenter's study.

Hood's delay in launching the Tennessee Campaign, as highlighted at Decatur, Alabama, on October 26 through 29, 1864, was the result of his constant change of plans dictated by the lack of supplies. It was also due to the absence of General Nathan Bedford Forrest's cavalry, which was ordered to report to Hood on October 21, but did not fully arrive until November 14.

The series of failures of Hood's 1864 Tennessee Campaign began not at Spring Hill, Tennessee, on November 29, but six weeks earlier on the plains of northern Alabama. Hood's original post-Atlanta plan to invade Tennessee was to cross the Tennessee River at Guntersville, Alabama, and then march west to Tuscumbia, where supplies for the invasion would be

---

[3] Wiley Sword, *The Confederacy's Last Hurrah: The Battles of Spring Hill, Franklin, and Nashville* (1993), 65, 70, 74, 75.

waiting. Reports of stronger than expected Union defenses at Guntersville forced Hood to change his plans and move to Decatur, which, according to intelligence, had only a small garrison of 1,750. Hood tested the Decatur defenses for three days before yielding to the defiant bluecoats and striking west to attempt a crossing at Courtland. By this time there were no supplies, and the whereabouts of Forrest's cavalry was still unknown.

Hood arrived at Courtland on October 29. Still without supplies, Hood moved out the next day for Tuscumbia, which he reached on November 1. He decided to wait there for Forrest and supplies before continuing on. Forrest and his horsemen arrived three weeks later, and Hood started the invasion on November 22. General Thomas, meanwhile, organized and trained in preparation to meet the oncoming Confederates.

Thanks to Noel Carpenter, Civil War scholarship now has a meticulously researched and efficiently presented chronicle of the crucial events that have been heretofore overshadowed by the bookends of the Atlanta and Tennessee campaigns. This new printing by Savas Beatie of *Detour to Disaster* will gain a wider audience than the first privately printed edition.

Stephen M. Hood

Author of *John Bell Hood: The Rise, Fall, and Resurrection of a Confederate General* (2013) and editor of *The Lost Papers of Confederate General John Bell Hood* (2016)

FOREWORD
TO THE 2000 EDITION

The author of this contribution to the study of Civil War history was my father, Noel Carpenter. He did not live to see it in print, but he did complete the manuscript before his death in December of 2000 at age 82. He might have wanted to do more wordsmithing, but nevertheless I hope he would have been happy with how his book turned out. (Actually I can picture his face lighting up like a football stadium.)

The only editing I did was for grammatical continuity.

Carol Carpenter Powell

For the past twelve years I have been pursuing a curiosity about the Civil War action in Decatur, Alabama, which took place a few blocks from my home and in many of the places where I played as a boy. My main interest was the fighting on the ground as the soldiers saw it. Endless searching for this scarce lore turned up facets of the engagement of more significance, and I began to agree with Colonel Doolittle's belief that it deserved more attention than it has received in the war's history. I decided to write about it, and this account is the result.

General Hood's changes of strategy that brought him to Decatur made the events at this stage of the Tennessee Campaign a turning point with many important implications. His own account of those developments hints of rationalization and leaves his true intentions still unclear. General Sherman, as he tried to find a way to cross the river and reach Nashville, was trying to withdraw from the area and get back to his plan for crossing Georgia, while General Thomas desperately sought to form a defense line in Tennessee. The interaction of these strategies on two fronts in this classic setting where the river, the railroads and the telegraph lines played such a large part, makes this affair a case study for students of strategy. General Hood's confused battlefield tactics and the many problems that engulfed him at Decatur seemed to foretell the future of the campaign.

The circumstances of this early part of the Tennessee Campaign invite second-guessing of the decisions of both General Hood and General Sherman. I have tried to avoid doing that and will leave it to the reader to decide what would have happened if Hood and Sherman had done this or that thing differently. Both of these generals made mistakes that are forcefully revealed in this account. Since his campaign failed, General Hood's mistakes are more notable but my judgment of his performance is tempered with empathy because of the difficulty of the circumstances he faced.

The people who helped me with this manuscript by encouragement and other more direct ways are too numerous to mention fully. With apologies for omissions, I wish to thank Maurice J. Jones, an expert on the subject, who led me to some rare sources and generously gave access to his own manuscript; the late Winston S. Garth, Jr. and A. Julian Harris who gave me valuable source books; Rev. William D. Simrell for long and continual encouragement; the University of Texas at Austin libraries and the Interlibrary Loan Service for superior service; Carol and Gary Powell, my daughter and son-in-law, who gave me guidance and encouragement; and last but not least, my wife Betty, who put up with papers and general clutter for a good many years.

Noel Carpenter

Austin, Texas
October 2000

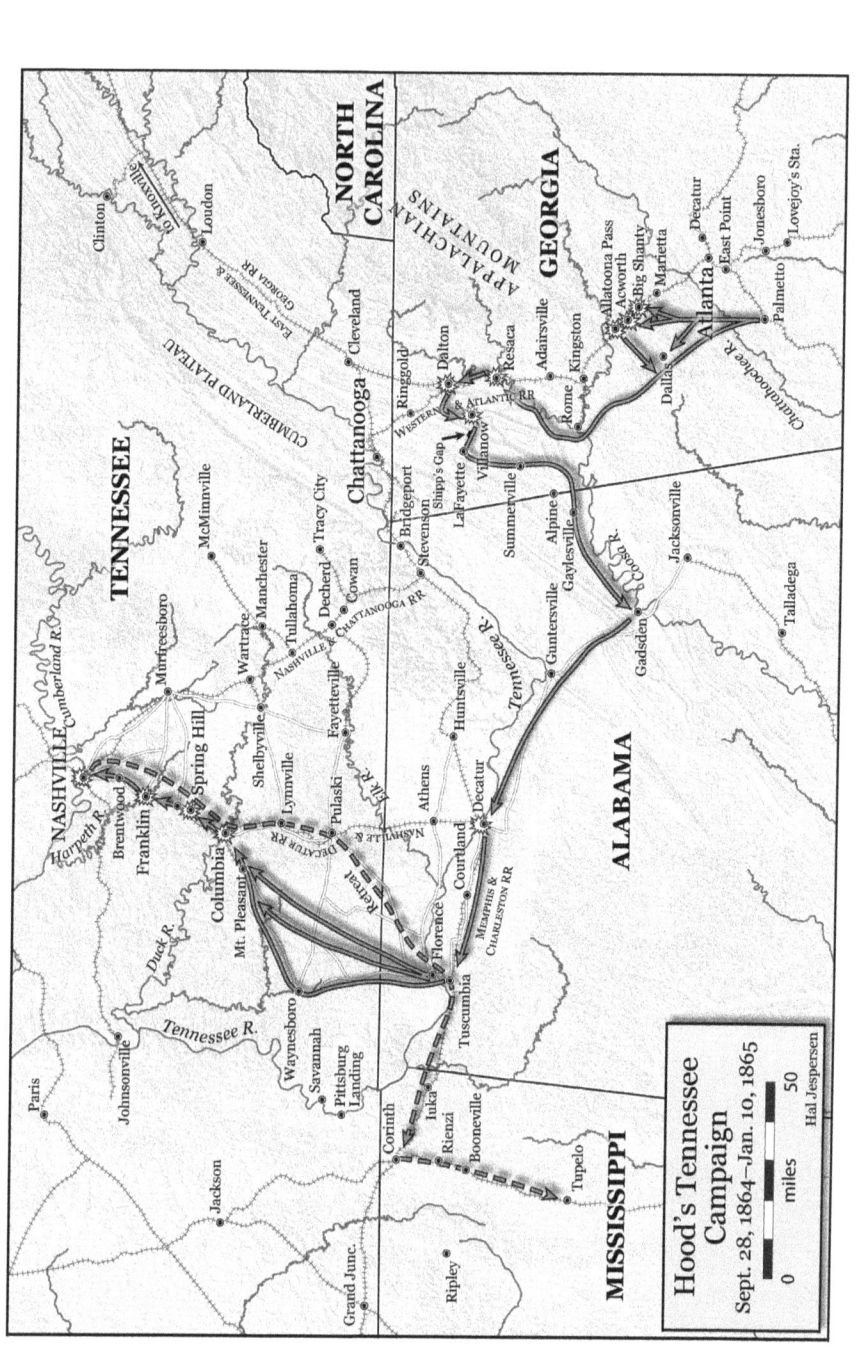

Hood's Tennessee
Campaign
Sept. 28, 1864–Jan. 10, 1865

Hal Jespersen

0   miles   50

CHAPTER ONE

Prelude — Fall of Atlanta

ENERAL JOHN BELL HOOD'S STRATEGY FOR THE opening move of the Tennessee Campaign in 1864 was plausible, even promising to some observers — "dashing in the extreme," in the words of Lord Wolseley, General Viscount, Adjutant General of the British Army.[1] He would cross the Tennessee River at or near Guntersville and capture the railroad junction at Stevenson. From this key position he could march to Nashville and defeat Maj. Gen. George H. Thomas while blocking reinforcements from General Sherman's main armies at Gaylesville, Alabama. When he abruptly diverted to Decatur on 23 October after one day's march from Gadsden, his plan began to unravel. So many problems developed from the new route that the stout resistance put up by the fort at Decatur seemed to tip the scales against a river crossing there, and he abandoned this strategy. It was a turning point that changed the nature of the campaign and momentarily caused Hood to despair of ever reaching Nashville.

In some other campaign or some other war this four-day fight might be counted as a major event. In fact, General Granger's estimate of Confederate casualties would place it among the 149 important battles of the war as measured by casualties. But not in the desperate mood of the Tennessee

Campaign. In the company of the catastrophic battles at
Franklin and Nashville, it has been almost forgotten in the
battle lore of the war. While it doesn't rank high for combat
action, it must be near the top of the scale in terms of the
complexity of the military problems faced by the young
Confederate commander and in the weight of its consequences. The troubles with grand tactics, supply, transportation, artillery, cavalry and communications that converged on
the Army of Tennessee at Decatur would have challenged the
shrewdest of generals. To a lesser degree this could be said of
Sherman's calculations for balancing his forces between the
defense of Tennessee and his campaign across Georgia.
General Thomas' problem was simpler but, for him, in-
tractable: he had to have reinforcements to be able to stop
Hood from reaching Nashville, while Sherman stubbornly
held on to two-thirds of the Union's western armies for his
own purposes. Hood's reputation among his critics as a sort of
bungler began here, yet Sherman virtually escaped censure for
erring at the same time on a grander scale by leaving General
Thomas in a position from which only the fortunes of war
saved him.[2]

At the time the Army of Tennessee reached Decatur, the
fort there was only a few months old and the defensive works
were still being perfected. Early in 1864 General Grant was
commander of the Union's Military Division of the Mississippi at Chattanooga. In his plans for a spring offensive
against Atlanta he wanted to improve his tenuous supply lines
from Nashville, which depended almost entirely on the single-
track Nashville-Chattanooga railroad. To prepare for an alter-
nate route he gave Brig. Gen. Grenville M. Dodge at Athens

the responsibility for keeping the rail line open from Nashville to Decatur Junction and from there to Stevenson. For this to be successful, General Dodge knew he would need to capture and control the town of Decatur to help defend against the frequent Confederate cavalry raids being made against the railroad north of the river. On 7 March he led a brigade of infantry from Athens on a night crossing of the river just upstream from Decatur and easily captured the town the next morning. He designated the post as Detachment, Fourth Division, Sixteenth Army Corps, and put Brig. Gen. John D. Stevenson in command. General Stevenson immediately laid a pontoon bridge anchored to the pilings of the burned-out bridge on the Memphis and Charleston railroad line. By 23 March he had constructed two artillery redoubts and evacuated the citizens (see Appendix C). Later the town had been encircled with a breast-high embankment and an outer defense line of rifle pits with two fortified positions for artillery on the east side.[3]

On 9 March General Grant was promoted and given command of all Union forces. He chose Maj. Gen. William T. Sherman to replace him as commander of the Military Division of the Mississippi, made up of the Union's western armies — Army of the Ohio, Army of the Tennessee and Army of the Cumberland, each with two corps. Grant quickly broadened his spring offensive plans to include attacks against the Confederate forces on all fronts. In one of the two largest offensive thrusts, he would supervise Maj. Gen. George G. Meade's Army of the Potomac in an attack on Gen. Robert E. Lee's Army of Northern Virginia with Richmond as the objective. Simultaneously, General Sherman was to push his armies against Gen. Joseph E. Johnston's Army of Tennessee in Georgia to break it up and sever the Confederacy on a line to Mobile or Savannah. Grant launched his attack across the Rapidan River on 4 May and struck at Lee in some of the bloodiest battles of the war — The Wilderness, Spottsylvania, New Market, Cold Harbor and several others. Lee repulsed his direct attacks, inflicting heavy Union losses, but he continued to move around Lee's right flank. Finally Lee fortified at Petersburg, and Grant's offensive ended. This thirty-day campaign had cost 50,000 Union and 32,000 Confederate casualties. Both armies were tied down in a prolonged trench warfare which continued almost to the end of the war. Although he hadn't taken Richmond, Grant had succeeded in immobilizing Lee and preventing any cooperation between him and the Army of Tennessee.[4]

Meanwhile, General Sherman moved his army from Chattanooga on 16 May to Dalton, Georgia, where the Army of Tennessee had been in winter camp, and struck at Johnston in the battle of Rocky Face Ridge. Outgunned and outnumbered two to one, General Johnston began a defensive campaign in which he slowly fell back toward Atlanta, giving battle from prepared positions only when it was advantageous. He continued this pattern, inflicting punishing casualties on the Union forces in battles at Resaca, Newhope Church, Kennesaw Mountain and Big Shanty. Confederate President Jefferson Davis grew increasingly dissatisfied with these Fabian tactics until finally, with the army in distant sight of Atlanta, he made the grave decision to relieve Johnston in mid-campaign. His choice of a replacement commander was shocking to the men and officers of the army who loved and trusted Johnston. Passing over Lt. Gen. William J. Hardee, the senior and most respected corps commander, he picked Lt. Gen. John B. Hood. Hood had a record for boldness and aggressiveness and was a strong believer in offensive tactics, just what the president believed was needed. At 33 Hood would be the youngest full general in the Confederacy. (This was a temporary rank in the Provisional Army, Confederate States pending confirmation of promotion in the regular CSA by the legislature. It was not confirmed by the war's end.)[5]

Hood's distinguished combat record as commander of the renowned Texas Brigade at Second Manassas and Antietam and of a division at Gettysburg and Chickamauga had made him a Confederate hero. He had earned a reputation as the bravest of the brave. The sling holding up his withered left arm and his empty right trouser leg testified to the wounds he had received at Gettysburg and Chickamauga. When he rode his horse "Jeff Davis" he needed the help of two aides to mount and then be strapped to the saddle. Although he was in pain most of the time it didn't seem to dull his determination. But most of his officers and men were less impressed with these charismatic qualities than they were concerned with another persistent reputation he had for rashness and immature judgment.[6]

True to President Davis' expectations, Hood attacked the Union army in three major battles on the outskirts of Atlanta in late July — Peachtree Creek, Decatur (Battle of Atlanta) and Ezra Church. In ten days he had lost 18,000 casualties, nearly one-third of the force he had taken over. These valiant efforts only delayed Sherman's larger army. Hood was forced to withdraw to the south on 31 August, leaving Atlanta in Union hands. Paradoxically, up until this loss, it was said the Confederacy was as near to independence and a kind of victory in the war as it had ever been. The huge Union casualty lists which had filled northern newspapers for months so appalled the northern people that Lincoln's defeat in the approaching election was a near certainty. Democratic candidate George B. McClellan was heavily favored to win the presidency on a platform which seemed to promise a cease fire and negotiated peace. When Sherman announced his victory — "Atlanta is ours and fairly won" — it was like a tonic to the people.[7] Public opinion swung in support of the war, and Lincoln's opposition vanished almost overnight.[7a]

For this victory General Sherman became the man of the hour. He had accomplished a major step in Grant's objective to further divide the Confederacy. The capture of Vicksburg in July 1863 had already cut away the Trans-Mississippi states, Louisiana, Arkansas and Texas, from the western arena. Now, with the Union in possession of Atlanta, one of the two rail lines supplying food to Lee's army was closed, and Sherman was within reach of both Mobile and Savannah. Union soldiers enjoyed a brief period of fame while they turned to the easier duties of occupying Atlanta and absorbing the fresh regiments and supplies pouring in.

General Hood fell back to Lovejoy's Station, then on 19 September to Palmetto, thirty miles southwest of Atlanta. Here his battered army camped for nearly two weeks while he waited for supplies to be accumulated at Blue Mountain near what is now Anniston, Alabama. Due to the heavy casualties in the battles around Atlanta, it was an army much diminished from its former strength, and there was almost no hope of reinforcements. Clear signs of low morale showed in the men. Their uniforms were ragged and threadbare, and thousands were bare-footed. Hood's quartermaster, Col. M.B. McMicken, had destroyed his reserve supply train while withdrawing from Atlanta. Eighty-seven carloads, including twenty-eight cars of ammunition, were lost. Hood blamed this on Colonel McMicken's drinking habits. A seven-dollar pay raise from eleven to eighteen dollars a month had been authorized in June, but the men hadn't been paid since February anyway. Desertions were at a high level as many men, believing the cause was hopeless, went home to take care of their families.[8]

Despite these signs no one doubted that this was still a powerful army of patriots and hardened veterans. "There were no sick, and the health of the Army was admirable. The men had learned to take care of themselves under the most trying circumstances and were capable of almost any amount of endurance. I doubt if the ranks of any army were ever composed of better material or could be more relied on in an emergency."[9] Such was the assessment of Brig. Gen. Arthur M. Manigault of Lee's Corps.

Sherman made no effort to pursue him, and Hood let his men rest at Palmetto while he tried to develop some plan to rescue the Confederacy. With pitifully few alternatives open to him he chose one which would have an immediate effect on Sherman's operations and some promise of reversing his victory at Atlanta. Sherman was at the end of a 105-mile supply line over a one-track railroad from his supply depots in Chattanooga and Nashville. Every day 130 carloads of supplies had to come down this track to sustain the Union army. Without them Sherman would be crippled. Hood decided to move north and attack this line to force Sherman to turn back on him. He expected Sherman to divide his army to do this, leaving a considerable part of it in Atlanta. With their strengths more nearly equalized he hoped to bring on a battle near the Alabama line and defeat Sherman "in detail." He outlined his plan in a dispatch to Richmond on the twenty-second.[10]

President Davis came to Palmetto on 25 September to inspect the Army, and Hood had a chance to present his proposed strategy at length. The president approved of the plan and made it official by letter from Montgomery on the twenty-eighth, but by then he had hedged a bit. He wrote that he had decided to combine the forces of Hood's Department of Tennessee and Georgia with those of Lt. Gen. Richard Taylor's Department of Alabama, Mississippi and East Louisiana. He expected to appoint Gen. P.G.T. Beauregard to head the new command, which would be designated as the Military Division of the West. The Army of Tennessee would then be under a single theater commander along with Maj. Gen. Nathan B. Forrest's cavalry corps and Brig. Gen. Phillip D. Roddey's cavalry division. Davis' instructions to Beauregard, however, were equivocal and seemed to make him more an advisor than a commander. Since Hood had already discussed his plans with the president, Beauregard was inhibited and unsure of his authority over Hood's course.[11]

The president had hoped in this way to add Beauregard's mature judgment to Hood's aggressiveness, but this was not to be. Hood was to ignore or avoid Beauregard's guidance almost from the start. In the days after this, President Davis made several public speeches pretty much revealing Hood's plan, along with some elaborations of his own. This information reached General Sherman almost immediately from newspaper accounts and from a spy who was present when the president addressed Hood's men.[12]

For the next three weeks General Hood moved the Army of Tennessee northward. Bit by bit during this time he developed the strategy of what was to become the Tennessee Campaign. While reluctantly pursuing Hood, General Sherman concentrated more and more on his own plan for cutting loose from his supply line and moving across Georgia.

CHAPTER TWO

Hood Turns North

THE ARMY OF TENNESSEE LEFT PALMETTO ON 29 September, following a looping course along the path it had come down under General Johnston a few months before. Hood moved toward Dalton, attacking garrisons along the railroad and destroying some thirty miles of track which completely disrupted Sherman's communications for a time. As soon as he discovered Hood's movement, Sherman put his army in pursuit on 3 October, as Hood had predicted. But he dashed Hood's hope that he would split his forces. Leaving only the Twentieth Corps at Atlanta, he brought all five of the remaining corps with him. The balance of forces hardly changed. Believing Hood would head for Blue Mountain and the Gadsden area where he would be a threat to Tennessee, Sherman sent Maj. Gen. George H. Thomas to Nashville to guard against that danger and to drive Forrest's cavalry out of Tennessee.[1]

Thomas, a Virginian who had remained loyal to the Union, was a consistently effective and dependable general and probably the best of Sherman's commanders. He had earned the title "Rock of Chickamauga" for his heroic stand in that battle and had commanded the Army of the Cumberland in the Atlanta Campaign. Sherman's order on 3 October directed him to take command of all the forces in Tennessee and

to hold defensively Nashville, Chattanooga, and Decatur, Alabama. Sherman calculated that the troops available to
Thomas and already in Tennessee would total 45,000 men. To
these he planned to add the two divisions of Maj. Gen. A.J.
Smith's Sixteenth Corps then in Missouri. These eight to ten
thousand men were on detached service to Maj. Gen. William
S. Rosecrans' Department of Missouri helping to drive the
Confederate forces out of Missouri. Sherman decided that he
would also send his own 4th Corps to Thomas later, if necessary. On paper this seemed a reasonable troop strength for
Thomas' mission.[2]

At first General Thomas couldn't disagree with Sherman's
assessment, but after he reached Nashville and took a closer
look he had a rude awakening. Of the 20,000 troops there,
10,000 were cavalry without horses. They had been dismounted to furnish horses for General Kilpatrick's cavalry
division that went with Sherman. Thomas considered some of
them "little better than militia."[3] The other 10,000 men were
convalescents from the Atlanta Campaign — "the sick,
wounded and worthless," as Sherman called them — and
some new inexperienced regiments.[4] In addition there were a
number of civilian employees of the Quartermaster Corps
who could be armed and used for defense. Thomas' only effective field force was 7,700 cavalry watching General Forrest's
cavalry along the Tennessee River near Florence. The rest of
his force consisted of small garrisons at Chattanooga, Murfreesboro, and North Alabama and at scattered
posts along the railroads. To make things worse, he found
some unexpected leaks in his troop strength which were
becoming quite substantial. Because of the approaching

elections he was required to send whole regiments of men back to their home states to vote. Also about this time the three-year term of service was beginning to expire with increasing regularity in his veteran regiments, and they had to be sent home for discharge. General Thomas ruefully concluded that he was far from ready to stop Hood if he turned into Tennessee with an army of 40,000 battle-hardened veterans — the same army which, he said, "had so skillfully resisted the advance of the whole active army of the Military District of the Mississippi from Dalton to the Chattahoochee."[5]

At this time the Union post at Decatur was the head-quarters of the District of North Alabama, Army of the Cumberland. Brig. Gen. Robert S. Granger (FIG. 2) was commander of the district, reporting directly to General Thomas, and Col. Charles C. Doolittle (FIG. 9) of the Eighteenth Michigan Infantry commanded the post. A West Point class-mate of General Beauregard from the class of 1838, Granger was an experienced career officer with a long period of service in the Mexican War and at forts on the Texas frontier. He had been promoted to Brigadier General of Volunteers in 1862. He was responsible for protecting the Memphis and Charles-ton railroad from Decatur to Stevenson and for defending the Decatur, Athens and Huntsville area.[6]

When General Thomas asked for a strength report on 8 October, Granger replied that he had 1,200 men at Decatur and 300 at Athens. With this force he could only man half of the 1,600-yard length of his defensive works at Decatur, he said. His 840 infantry would cover just one man to two yards of front. (One textbook standard for defense of a fort called for one and a half to two men per yard.) This was the first of several pleas for reinforcement Granger was to make, but General Thomas wasn't ready to shift any of his limited forces until Hood's objective and route became clearer. In the end he almost waited too long.[7]

The fort at Decatur surrounded the center of town and extended to the river on both sides. It consisted of an earthen, breast-high parapet nearly a mile long fronted by a ditch and lined with logs and gabions — open-ended baskets of woven branches filled with dirt and rocks. An artillery redoubt entirely enclosed by breastworks was located at the southern apex of the works. It was called Fort No. 2. A slightly smaller, more elongated redoubt containing a small blockhouse was located at the western shoulder of the enclosure and designated as Fort No. 1. Both positions had embrasures for fourteen guns. Sally ports were located at each end of Fort No. 1 and each side of Fort No. 2 where the fort parapet joined the artillery works. Embrasures for four guns were distributed to the left and right in the fort parapet, and a small interior redoubt was located toward the west part of the line. In addition, a small artillery redoubt was located 800 yards to the east on the Somerville Road, and a small earthwork was about 300 yards north of it. A line of rifle pits connected these positions and extended to the north and south. The south and west faces of the fort were well ditched and protected by a barrier line of abatis. These felled trees with their sharpened branches pointing outward the same purpose as barbed wire was to do in later times. The eastern face was not as strong and, Col. Doolittle thought, would have been difficult to hold against a determined attack by a large force.[8]

The ground around the town was very favorable for defense, generally falling slightly away from the fort with no elevated points in the vicinity to serve as lodgements for an enemy's artillery. As General Granger described it, "The country about the fort for 800 yards is entirely unobstructed. At that distance it is intersected by a ravine and water course beginning on the left [east] and running across the Somerville, Moulton and Courtland roads. Beyond the ravine the ground rises in a sparsely wooded slope for 700 yards and is bounded by a dense wood stretching across our entire front and bending northward finds the river at a distance of 1,000 yards upon our right."[9] By October the town was nearly depopulated, and all but a few of the houses had been burned or torn down.[10]

While Hood moved to the northwest, attacking then drawing back from the railroad, the federal high command all the way up to General Grant and President Lincoln were speculating about his intentions. General Sherman changed his opinion almost daily between the possibilities that Hood would cross the Tennessee River or turn south toward Blue Mountain, the terminus of the Alabama and Tennessee River Railroad from Selma. From there the Confederate army could be supplied indefinitely by rail from the south and move to Tennessee or threaten the Union rear if Sherman turned to the east.

As he tracked Hood from Nashville, General Thomas had another concern almost as worrisome. He was responsible for containing Forrest's cavalry that was already threatening west Tennessee from Corinth and Tuscumbia. On 23 September Forrest had made a spectacular raid against the railroad line from Athens to Pulaski, capturing the fort at Athens and the blockhouses along the tracks, and destroying the bridges and trestles. On 8 October General Thomas directed Maj. Gen. Lovell H. Rousseau, commander of the Union's District of Tennessee, to destroy every ferry boat and crossing on the river between Decatur and Eastport, Mississippi, and if possible find out where Forrest was. For Rousseau the job of locating Forrest was largely guesswork because of the almost constant movement of Brig. Gen. Phillip D Roddey's cavalry division across the Tennessee Valley.[11]

On the seventh, General Hood dispatched an urgent request to General Taylor to have Forrest's cavalry operate against the railroads in Tennessee as far east as the Nashville-Chattanooga line. Pursuing the notion of cutting Sherman's communications further north, he changed his plan the next day in what he called an afterthought. He decided that after battling Sherman, he would cross the river near Guntersville and capture Stevenson and Bridgeport. By breaking Sherman's supply pipeline there he expected to draw him further from Georgia. On the ninth, he sent a dispatch to Richmond asking Gen. Braxton Bragg, the president's military advisor, to have the railroad repaired from Tuscumbia to Decatur. This would establish another line for supplies and in case of defeat in his expected battle with Sherman's army. Whatever action Bragg took to accomplish this was overtaken by events, and nothing was done.[12]

On 11 October, General Granger again requested reinforcements. His works at Decatur were very extensive and by no means formidable, he said, and with the present strength could be taken by 10,000 men without great loss. Also, the

lake on the north side of the river there made a potential trap
that would keep him from holding the strip of land between
the lake and the river. Brig. Gen. John T. Croxton, whose
Union cavalry brigade was at Decatur that same day, described
this lake as deep and narrow, running parallel with the river
200 to 400 yards from it and extending two miles. Granger
requested 2,000 more men.[13]

On the fourteenth, General Granger reported to General
Thomas that the U.S. Army gunboat *Stone River* and the
Navy gunboat *General Thomas* were making daily reconnaissance trips out of Decatur and reporting the usual enemy
activity up the river, some 500 to 600 Confederates being
sighted. He was contemptuous of these all-wood gunboats
for defensive use. As he wrote General Thomas on the sixteenth, they would do little toward stopping a force such as
Hood's from crossing the river. "They have no protection for
their boilers, none indeed for any part of the boat, and any
of them could be totally disabled by three batteries in fifteen minutes."[14]

The *Stone River* was assigned full time to Granger's
control and was manned by army men under Capt. W.A.
Naylor of the Tenth Ohio Artillery. A stern-wheeler of 214
tons capacity, it was the second largest boat built at Bridgeport during the war. The smaller *General Thomas* was one of
four side-wheel gunboats built at Bridgeport for the Navy.
These four formed the Upper Tennessee Fleet of the Mississippi Squadron, Eleventh Naval District. The *General Thomas*
mounted six guns, two twenty-pounder Parrott rifles on the
bow and two twenty-four-pounder howitzers on each side. It
was captained by Acting Master Gilbert Morton. A nearly

identical sister ship, the *General Sherman* (FIG. 3), and two slightly larger boats, the *General Grant* and the *General Burnside*, made up the rest of the fleet at Bridgeport. Lt. Moreau Forrest commanded the four-boat fleet from his flagship the *General Burnside*.[15]

Despite his grave concerns General Granger left Decatur on the sixteenth and went to Huntsville where his wife was staying. That night they called on Col. William P. Lyon of the Thirteenth Wisconsin Infantry and his wife. Lyon, the Huntsville post commander, noted that Granger was "very salubrious" and observed that his family was quite popular in Huntsville. His treatment of the regiment was kind and considerate as well, Lyon said. Mrs. W.D. Chadick, a Huntsville resident, had met General Granger that summer and said he was a very dignified, courteous gentleman who treated her very well.[16]

The Army of Tennessee was highly visible yet elusive as it zigzagged along the Atlanta-Chattanooga Railroad. On 8 October at Cedartown, Georgia, General Hood sent two-thirds of his artillery and most of the wagon train under Maj. Gen. Arnold Elzey, his chief of artillery, to a new temporary supply base at Jacksonville, Alabama. Men with no shoes and the walking sick and wounded were sent along with the train. For most of these men it was a welcome respite, since they weren't made to march in formation and could get along at their own pace. They called this the "slow train."[17]

With the corps stripped of impediments Hood moved them on separate missions to attack the railroad line. While Stewart's Corps attacked Big Shanty, Acworth and Alatoona,

Hood marched north with the other two corps, circling to the west of Rome, and sent Lee's Corps to destroy the tracks at Resaca, bypassing Resaca which refused to surrender. Hood himself took Cheatham's Corps and captured Dalton. These were not difficult victories, except for Alatoona where a million rations of bread and other supplies were stored. General Stewart sent French's Division to take the place and destroy the stores, but through an odd set of circumstances the mission failed. In the middle of a severe fight against the 2,000 defenders of a makeshift fort, General French (FIG. 6) had to withdraw because of a false report of an enemy force approaching his rear. The attack cost the division 799 casualties which, with the 700 Union losses, made it one of the more bloody fights of the war for the number engaged. Final efforts to burn the supplies were thwarted when no matches could be found to start a fire. General Cockrell had three matches, but when the men tried to strike them they would not ignite.[18]

To the Union Commanders Hood's forces seemed to be everywhere. Sherman was flooded with reports from all directions telling of suspected Rebel sightings, but he couldn't pinpoint either Hood's position or his objective. In a 7 October dispatch to General Corse he seemed to blame Hood for his own confusion: "He is an eccentric and I cannot guess his movements as I could those of Johnston, who was a sensible man and only did sensible things."[19] On 11 October the reports suddenly stopped, and for a brief time the Confederate army couldn't be located anywhere. By the seventeenth, Sherman thought Hood might be headed for Tennessee to the west of Huntsville, but later in the day he wrote to General

Thomas, "Hood won't go into Tennessee. I hope he will ....
The gunboats can break any bridge he may attempt above
Decatur. If he attempts to cross let him do so in part, and then
let a gunboat break through his bridge .... I will follow him to
Gadsden, and then I want my whole army united for the
grand move into Georgia. He cannot maintain his army north
of the Tennessee."[20]

On the same day General Granger was watching for signs
of Hood's advance at Decatur, but all he could report was that
a Mrs. Gill of Somerville had told scouts that no Confederate troops were there. Also, one of his scouts just in from
Courtland said General Roddey was sick at his home in
Moulton and his cavalry command was en route from Tuscumbia to Courtland.[21]

On the nineteenth, Sherman wrote Maj. Gen. Henry
W. Halleck, Grant's Chief of Staff in Washington, with the
ambiguous advice that Hood would not venture toward Tennessee except around by Decatur. A little later he wrote
to Halleck again, saying he thought Hood would move to
Blue Mountain, and added, "I now consider myself authorized to execute my plan to ... strike out for the heart of
Georgia."[22] This was confident language, but he knew it was
General Grant he had to convince and Grant still wanted
him to destroy Hood's army as his first priority. He must
have known that everything he said to Halleck would soon
be known to Grant who was at City Point, Virginia. He
seemed to be using Halleck as an indirect channel to influence
Grant's position.[23]

On the twenty-first Sherman telegraphed some of his
perplexity with Hood in a message to General Thomas: "To

pursue Hood is folly, for he can twist and turn like a fox and wear out any army in pursuit .... I think he will follow me, at least with his cavalry, in which event I want you to push south from Decatur ... for Columbus, Mississippi and Selma."[24]

CHAPTER THREE

Tennessee Campaign Strategy

B Y THE TIME THEY ARRIVED AT CROSS ROADS, GEORGIA, on 15 October the Confederate soldiers had been on the march constantly for more than two weeks. General Hood called a two-day halt while the men rested. Up to now his plans hadn't gone beyond bringing Sherman to battle and breaking his supply pipeline to Nashville. In the days at Cross Roads he developed the idea of extending his objective into a strategy of wider consequence for the war. After consulting his corps commanders, he decided not to battle Sherman as he had planned. Instead he determined, as before, to cross the Tennessee River at Guntersville and cut Sherman's communications by taking the railroad junction at Stevenson while his cavalry destroyed the bridge at Bridgeport. Then, with General Thomas cut off from reinforcement by Sherman, he would move to Nashville along the line of the Nashville-Chattanooga Railroad and defeat Thomas before he could organize a defense. This, he reasoned, would force Sherman to follow him to middle Tennessee to protect his line of communications and his supply depots at Nashville. Georgia would be free from Union control. He could recruit more men in Tennessee and, after defeating Thomas, move into Kentucky to threaten Cincinnati. From there he could move east to reinforce Lee's army at Richmond.[1]

The key to the first part of this plan was the rail line from Stevenson to Nashville. If Hood controlled it, Sherman could only chase the army from behind and couldn't easily join or reinforce General Thomas. He would be cut off from the vast supply depot at Nashville. If necessary, Hood could escape to the west with one of his objectives accomplished; Sherman would be back in Tennessee. Any other route to Nashville which Hood might take would give Sherman these advantages in reverse. He could move ahead of Hood by rail and block him or attack his right flank from Murfreesboro or anywhere along the route, perhaps trapping him north of the river.

This was the strategy of what was to become the Tennessee Campaign. It would mean moving rapidly and without a supply base, at least for some length of time. Once the army was across the river, Jacksonville would be vulnerable to the enemy in Georgia and eastern Alabama and untenable as a base. Hood decided to move his base to Tuscumbia, as he said, in case of his defeat in Tennessee and a retreat in that direction. It would be his only source for ammunition resupply. He planned to order a heavy reserve of artillery so that he could counter the enemy's gunboats long enough to allow him to recross the river in case of emergency. (Apparently he never did this.)[2]

A critical element in these considerations was the close proximity of the Union Army, which was highlighted just then by a message from General Wheeler. A dispatch from him on 16 October reported that Sherman was in full force at Snake Creek Gap, fifteen miles away.[3]

The army took up the march to Gadsden where it arrived on 20 October and went into camp. It was rejoined there by the men, artillery and wagons left at Jacksonville. General Beauregard arrived at Gadsden at 11:00 a.m. the same day, and he and Hood discussed the new strategy the rest of that day and all the next. One of the reasons Hood gave for his plan to cross the river at Guntersville was that he had thoroughly destroyed the railroad near Marietta and Dalton. He could destroy the bridge at Bridgeport and move the army into middle Tennessee before Sherman could repair the road below Chattanooga. He believed it would take five or six weeks to repair the tracks. Without the bridge, Sherman's troop movements to Stevenson would be slowed to marching speed, and he would have to build a pontoon bridge. His rail line for supplies from Chattanooga to the north side of the river would be cut off.[4]

Hood argued that the Mobile and Ohio Railroad from near Selma into Corinth, and the Memphis and Charleston from there to Tuscumbia, were in fair condition and could be improved before he was likely to need them. He believed he would have no trouble finding food provisions in middle Tennessee and also could capture supplies from the enemy. Beauregard thought the plan was bold and likely to lead to great results if carried out "fearlessly and, above all, judiciously," but he had misgivings about Hood's lack of the experience needed to carry it off. One of his main concerns was the lack of time to prepare a new supply base at Tuscumbia. With this reminder, Hood dispatched a message to General Taylor on the twentieth asking for his help in getting supplies to Tuscumbia.[5]

Hood had planned to take half of Maj. Gen. Joseph Wheeler's cavalry with the army and leave the rest behind to impede Sherman, but Beauregard insisted that all of the cavalry then in Georgia be left behind to do this. Only Jackson's Cavalry Division would go with the army. In return, Beauregard promised that he would instruct General Forrest and his cavalry to join Hood north of the river to guard the wagon trains. Hood readily agreed, since Wheeler's force had been badly cut up on a September raid through Tennessee and was in shabby condition and far under strength. According to General Beauregard, before Hood left Gadsden it was understood that his cavalry was to destroy the bridge at Bridgeport.[6]

As they were discussing this plan, the latest word from General Forrest, received on the twentieth, was that he was about to leave Corinth on the nineteenth for Clifton, Tennessee. He expected to contest a rumored river crossing by a Union division at Clifton Ferry. If he could defeat it, he would cross to the east bank of the river and destroy the Northwest Railroad to Nashville. On this basis Hood and Beauregard believed for nearly the next two weeks that Forrest was moving toward middle Tennessee. Although it might take a little time, this seemed to fit Hood's plan. Since he would be crossing the river at Guntersville with the wagons full, he wouldn't need a cavalry guard until he should establish a supply train to Tuscumbia for ordnance supply. Unfortunately, however, Forrest was unaware of Beauregard's intentions for him. He had already changed his plan and was at Jackson, Tennessee heading north on a raid.[7]

As General Beauregard concluded later, another bit of intelligence, this time from General Roddey, had an important influence on Hood's subsequent movements. Roddey reported on the eighteenth that there was only a small garrison at Decatur and no cavalry or enemy force north of the river from Florence to Decatur. All other force was believed going toward Bridgeport.[8]

Hood was satisfied when Beauregard approved his new strategy on 21 October. He detached Wheeler's Cavalry Corps and with it Ferguson's Brigade of Brig. Gen. William H. Jackson's cavalry division to stay in front of Sherman and delay his movements. Jackson was left with only Armstrong's and Ross's small brigades to accompany the army. In the long Atlanta Campaign these brigades had been reduced in strength to about the size of regiments. As Brig. Gen. Lawrence S. Ross wrote to a friend, his brigade had been in line of battle for 112 days straight and had fought eighty-six times during the Atlanta Campaign. His strength was down to just under 700 men after a loss of 303 men in killed, wounded and missing.[9]

The wagons that came up from Jacksonville brought a supply of shoes and clothing from the base there and a two-week accumulation of mail. Although quantities were far from adequate, shirts, socks, drawers, shoes and blankets were issued to the most needy men who were absolutely suffering for them. Two thousand men who were still barefooted were sent to the commissary's slaughter pens to fashion moccasins from fresh hides with the hair turned in. They wrapped their feet in old rags and sewed or tied the hide around them. These contraptions grew smelly from rot after a few days but usually stayed on until they wore out. Sometimes hard wrinkles formed in the skins as they dried and chafed the feet worse than walking barefooted.

Later, shops were established at brigade headquarters to reinforce worn-out shoes by sewing moccasins of hide over them.
Capt. Samuel T. Foster of the Twenty-Fourth Texas had his
shoes repaired this way and found them as comfortable as any
he ever had.[10]

Besides food and clothes, the wagons brought a supply
of ammunition which alleviated one of Hood's most severe
supply problems. After the loss of the army's supply train at
Atlanta, ammunition levels in the ordnance wagons and
caissons had been dangerously low. Instead of the 400 rounds
per artillery gun recommended for beginning a campaign,
Hood had started this one with only 106 per gun and no
reserve supply. Some of the shortage was made up at Gadsden,
and the caissons could proceed with a normal supply.
Ordnance remained a special problem, however, since there
was still no reserve source of resupply within reach. The
ammunition carried with the army in the ordnance wagons and caissons could be expended quickly in battle or in
reducing blockhouses along the railroad, and it couldn't
be obtained from civilian sources. A 12-pounder gun carried
128 rounds in its caissons and limbers and could be fired
easily at two rounds a minute even with careful aiming. (At
Franklin the Sixth Ohio Battery fired 550 rounds between
4:00 p.m. and dark on the first day.) General Hood had taken
a step toward providing a reserve on 23 September by asking the Ordnance Department to accumulate a large supply
of ammunition at Selma and Columbus or West Point,
Georgia, which they did. Stocks for the Tuscumbia base would
have to be shipped from Selma by rail then hauled in the
army's own wagons to the rear of the army.[11]

On Sunday the twentieth most of the men lay asleep nearly all day. At intervals wagons rolled in with supplies of clothes
and mail, and lines formed in the quartermaster's area as these
items were distributed. The camps took on a relaxed, almost
festive, atmosphere. French's Division of Stewart's Corps was
camped at Mrs. Sansom's farm two miles beyond Gadsden.
There, during the afternoon, General French arranged for a
band to play for Confederate heroine Emma Sansom and her
mother. In 1863 when she was sixteen, Emma had helped
General Forrest in his pursuit of a force of Union cavalry
raiders under Col. Abel D. Streight by guiding him to a ford
over Black Creek. The next day, 3 May, Forrest captured
Streight's entire force.[12]

In the late afternoon and on into the night of the twenty-
first, Hood and his commanders made the rounds of brigades
and regiments announcing the coming campaign. The loud
cheers and rebel yells which erupted from the men every few
minutes could be heard for miles. Most of them would be
moving closer to home for the first time in many months. For
all of them it would be good to be on the offensive again with
a chance to turn the tide of the war. As the Tennessee Campaign began, the morale of the army was the highest it had
been since Hood took command.[13]

While the Army of Tennessee was celebrating that afternoon, General Sherman reached Gaylesville, Alabama, just
thirty-five miles away with his Fourth and Fourteenth Corps
and made his bivouac in an open field back of the village.
He stationed the Fifteenth and Seventeenth Corps at Little
River and the Twenty-third Corps at Cedar Bluff. That night
he telegraphed General Grant that he didn't think Hood

would cross the river except at Muscle Shoals because of the gunboats at Bridgeport. All along, his defensive plans for the Tennessee River line had relied heavily on these boats, but their movements were already being restricted by low water on the river. The water level fell two inches in twenty-four hours on 24 October.[14]

Maj. Gen. David S. Stanley, commander of the Fourth Corps, recalled that Sherman stayed there in Gaylesville living in a tent like the rest of the ranking officers until 28 October. The march to the sea was decided upon here, and "for a week the plans and prospects of that march were discussed in a wall tent every day" while Sherman's senior commanders "sought wisdom and inspiration from short-stemmed pipes and sometimes a canteen of commissary whisky."[15] In these discussions there were several opinions but very little certainity as to what Hood would do. General Sherman thought he might move to Memphis and try to get control of the Mississippi River. To General Stanley it seemed that a march to the sea would be pretty safe for Sherman's army, but for the country and army left behind it was a tremendous risk. As he said later "Thomas was expected to beat Hood with one corps and two divisions. Sherman had failed to do this with six additional corps during an entire summer."[16]

The strength of the Army of Tennessee at this time was about 40,000 officers and men. The infantry was organized into three corps: Maj. Gen. Benjamin F. Cheatham's (FIG. 4) I Corps (11,600 men), Lt. Gen. Stephen D. Lee's II Corps (10,300 men), and Lt. Gen. Alexander P. Stewart's (FIG. 5) III Corps (11,600 men). These corps commanders were

competent and experienced officers, but they were all inexperienced at this level of command and had not yet acquired
the charismatic qualities of their predecessors. Cheatham,
known for his hard drinking and liberal use of profanity, had
been in command of his corps only since 28 September,
less than a month. He was selected against his wishes to
replace the veteran Lt. Gen. William J. Hardee whom Hood
had relieved because of his open opposition to Hood's leadership. (He had outranked Hood when Hood was promoted.)
Lee, the Confederacy's youngest lieutenant general at age
31, had taken over Hood's old corps when Hood took command of the Army in July. Stewart, affectionately known to
his men as "Old Straight," had the corps lately commanded
by the venerable Lt. Gen. Leonidas Polk who was killed
that June. Polk had been the Episcopal Bishop of Louisiana
before the war.[17]

Nine artillery battalions of three batteries each, four guns
to the battery, were evenly distributed among the corps, one
battalion per division. In addition, Jackson's Cavalry Division had two batteries of horse artillery that would accompany the army.[18]

With a twenty-day supply of rations in the wagons and the
men's haversacks, the army left Gadsden on 22 October on
an itinerary which would have taken it through Bennettsville, Cornelia, Brooksville and Red Hill to Warrenton near
Guntersville. Stewart's Corps took the lead and would force
the river crossing. Since he would be crossing a sizeable force
in pontoon boats to establish a bridgehead, most of the bridge
train followed him. Hood instructed General Stewart to move
at 2:00 a.m. with all his ordnance wagons and artillery, but as

to other trains to move just as they had been doing lately, leaving his food and baggage wagons to be handled by the army's quartermaster.[19]

He instructed General Wheeler with his cavalry to try to keep the railroad between Atlanta and Dalton constantly cut and to be prepared to join the main body of the army at any time if the enemy should evacuate Atlanta. If the enemy advanced anywhere, he was to drive off all livestock and destroy all the mills within ten miles of their line of march. General Jackson at Cave Springs, Georgia, forty miles east of Gadsden, was ordered to move his cavalry to the rear of the army as soon as possible and follow. Wagon trains under the quartermaster were to move with the army to Cornelia, then separate and go by Murfreesville and Blountsville to Oleander. On this circuitous route the wagons would be a long way from the army. It would be a race for the horses and men to catch up in time to follow the main body across the river.[20]

General Beauregard stayed behind to carry out his part in supporting Hood's plan. While the army marched away he sent a special messenger to General Taylor at Selma urging him to hasten supplies forward to Tuscumbia. Then in a preliminary order he instructed Taylor to have General Forrest and General Roddey enter into communication with Hood at some point between Guntersville and Decatur and to remain subject to Hood's orders. Surprisingly, in the same message he offered to send Jackson's cavalry to Taylor for protecting the railroads to Tuscumbia, if necessary. Hood would have had no cavalry at all with the army if Taylor had accepted, but he declined the offer. Later, Beauregard advised Richmond that the army had departed for the vicinity of Guntersville, circumstances to determine when and where it would cross the Tennessee River.[21]

The next day, 23 October, Beauregard sent General Taylor detailed orders for cooperating with Hood. A key part of his lengthy instructions was that Forrest should report to Hood in middle Tennessee "as soon as practicable after completing his current instructions."[22] This discretionary tone caused misunderstandings that were partly to blame for halting Hood's progress within a few days and were to haunt him for nearly two weeks. Other provisions of Beauregard's order put the entire responsibility for the supply of the Tuscumbia base and the railroad transportation to support it in Taylor's hands. He was instructed to transfer the supply base from Jacksonville to Tuscumbia and reroute all supplies there; to put the Mobile and Ohio and the Memphis and Charleston railroads in running order and supply them with rolling stock; to construct and man blockhouses for the protection of bridges and trestles and some other sizeable tasks.

General Taylor reacted immediately to part of this order on the twenty-third by directing General Roddey to repair the railroad. The same day he telegraphed Hood that trains were running from Corinth toward Tuscumbia and there was already a garrison at Corinth. But, as Hood was to find later, a fifteen-mile stretch of track near Tuscumbia was unusable, and trains could not reach there. Hood's plans and decisions were based on this misinformation for the next several days.[23]

Before winding up a long day of staff work on the twenty-third, Beauregard took care of a few other details. When the army crossed the Coosa River thirty-two miles from Rome, a pontoon bridge had been left behind and he arranged for it to be sent ahead to join Hood's bridge train. Then he wrote Hood with an idea he had for deceiving the enemy about the army's movement. He suggested that General Cheatham, a Tennessee native, sign an address to the people which would say he was coming to Tennessee to seek their cooperation while the main body of the army would destroy enemy lines between Chattanooga and Atlanta. By the time his dispatch reached Hood, he had already turned to the west. Apparently the idea was never carried out.[24]

On its line of march the army would be out of reach of the telegraph lines, which generally followed the railroads. The existing telegraph offices at Courtland, Decatur, Athens, Mooresville, Huntsville, Bridgeport and Stevenson were under enemy control. General Beauregard took steps to establish a courier detachment at Oxford, where the telegraph line from Selma ended, to deliver messages between General Taylor at Selma and the rear of the army. Couriers would ride the thirty miles from Oxford to Gadsden where Wheeler was located or to some connecting point on the courier line between Wheeler and Hood. This system might have helped, but after Hood turned west, it seemed to be confusing to everyone and was nearly useless.[25]

As they marched out of Gadsden on 22 October on the rocky dirt road toward Bennetsville, the soldiers noticed that there were hardly any men to be seen along the way. The women and children who were doing the labor in the fields appeared to be in destitute circumstances but seemed glad to see the army. In earlier days the soldiers were accustomed to women waving handkerchiefs and men cheering as they passed. Now they were moved and a bit puzzled when they saw that many of these ladies were shedding tears as they came out to greet acquaintances in the column. At the end of the day the army went into camps just west of Bennetsville with Hood's headquarters three and a half miles west of the post office there.[26]

As Hood reported later, it was here he learned that Forrest had not crossed the river, and he realized he couldn't proceed on this route without cavalry to guard the wagons in Tennessee. Believing high water on the river would prevent Forrest from crossing into middle Tennessee, he decided to move further down the river to meet him, as he recalled in his memoirs. But when he met General Beauregard at Decatur a few days later he gave Beauregard a different reason for his change of route. He said he had diverted to the west because he had reason to believe that the crossing point at Guntersville was too strongly guarded by the Federals. The nearest crossing point below there was Decatur, which he thought could be taken without great loss.[27]

Both of these were compelling reasons. For whatever reason, Forrest was not available, and Hood would need him sooner than he expected. With Sherman at Gaylesville, two or three days' march from Guntersville, a crossing there would be very risky. In the time it would take to bridge the river against even slight opposition, get the wagon train up and move the Army across, Sherman might catch up with them while the corps were separated by the river. As it turned out, this wasn't the threat it might have been. Sherman didn't know Hood had left Gadsden until the twenty-fifth.[28]

Orders were quickly changed for the new route of march. Hood ordered Cheatham to travel in light marching order like Stewart, leaving his food and baggage wagons with the quartermaster for better mobility. Vaughan's Brigade of Brown's Division was sent to Blountsville to meet and convoy the supply wagons and rejoin the army in the vicinity of Decatur. Since Lee's Corps would be in reserve, it would be moving in regular marching order with all of its wagons and artillery. Nevertheless, Lee sent the bulk of his artillery westward separately via Blountsville and Moulton to rejoin the corps west of Decatur. Each corps was accompanied by a pontoon bridge of some size. The Engineer Battalion had to allocate pontoons to streams along the way and still be able to concentrate for a river crossing.[29]

At this point an attack on the bridge at Bridgeport by Wheeler's Cavalry Corps might have succeeded. It would have had an added advantage as a diversion to screen the army's movements, but General Hood made no effort to do this. One reason must have been his belief that there would be plenty of time later while Sherman repaired the railroad to Chattanooga. But he had badly overestimated the time it would take to repair the tracks. Union engineers were already at work and would have the trains running through Chattanooga by 28 October. In any case, to Sherman at Gaylesville the railroad into Chattanooga was not as important as before. He could have marched his army to Bridgeport in a matter of days without going through Chattanooga. The line from Chattanooga running west through Bridgeport to Stevenson would now be most important to Sherman for supplying his army if he crossed to the north of the river.[30]

The Army of Tennessee marched to Brooksville on 23 October with the wagon train and Lee's artillery moving on parallel roads to the south. The next day at 7:00 a.m. it left Brooksville, taking the right hand road leading to Somerville, and marched to Blue Creek Church, nine miles from Somerville, a twenty-two mile march for the day. On the twenty-fifth, Hood and his staff arrived at Somerville at 11:00 a.m. and established headquarters in a lawyer's office. Stewart's Corps followed and camped immediately around town in the early afternoon. Maj. Gen. Edward C. Walthal's and Maj. Gen. William W. Loring's (FIG. 7) divisions halted just west of town on the Somerville-Decatur Road, and Maj. Gen. Samuel G. French's division stopped on the east side. Cheatham's Corps marched through town and turned left on the Cedar Plains Road to camp two miles from town. Lee's Corps remained back at Blue Creek Church, not moving during the day. As Loring's and Walthal's divisions passed through the town each regiment in turn was called to attention at right shoulder shift and marched down the street in parade fashion at close order. Loring's Division camped a half-mile from town.[31]

That night at the end of a twenty-seven mile march, the 700 wagons of the supply train slowly assembled in a number of camps near Blountsville. A commissary clerk in Walthal's Division who camped fourteen miles west of the town said the roads they traveled that day were the roughest he ever saw. Robert Patrick complained that this hard service was a constant thing and was wearing him down. They traveled hard all day until after dark "and then we must grope around in the darkness and find wood and water and by the time we cook our supper it is 12:00 o'clock and we must be up three hours before day."[32] When moving, the train stretched fifteen to twenty miles along the road, nearly a day's march between leading and trailing wagons. After the men went into camp they heard a good deal of firing which they supposed was at Decatur.[33]

Vaughan's Brigade, which was to escort the wagons, was already at Blountsville when the supply train arrived. Brig. Gen. George W. Gordon had been commanding the brigade since 4 July when Brig. Gen. Alfred J. Vaughan's foot was blown off by a shell near Atlanta. General Gordon noticed that most of the teams in the train were poor, jaded and looked half-starved. He deployed his men evenly among the wagons, and after hard marching on the following days, the men often pushing the wagons up hills and through creeks, they rejoined the Army near Courtland. The original route planned for the train would have taken it to Oleander to join the rear of the army. Whatever the reason for the change, it seemed to be the cause of the severe hunger of the men while they were at Decatur. Some of the wagons with corn for the horses were diverted to Decatur and reached the camps there on the twenty-eighth while the rest of the train continued to Courtland.[34]

For nearly three weeks the weather had been fair and pleasant, but that night a cold rain sent men scurrying for extra firewood and drew them closer to the camp fires. This was the beginning of one of the earliest and coldest winters this area had known for years. Capt. Evander M. Graham of the Twelfth Louisiana had complained in his diary just the night before that higher officials camped the troops too close together. Smoke from the many fires made it unpleasant in camp at night, and they could hardly see half the time, he wrote. Campfires were usually made about fifteen feet long so that three or four fires would accommodate a whole company. On this rainy night the fires were bigger than usual, but Graham probably felt less like complaining. He was from Downsville, Louisiana, and was the long-time commander of E Company, but at this time he was temporarily in command of the regiment. The Twelfth was one of the units that later made it to Johnston's army in North Carolina where Graham was promoted to Lieutenant Colonel and was in command of the regiment when it surrendered in 1865.[35]

This same day at Decatur General Granger telegraphed General Thomas that a scouting party toward Warrenton had found no Rebel force and that citizens south of the river could only place Hood somewhere between Gadsden and Blountsville. Messages he received from the *General Thomas* said enemy artillery and pontoons had been reported near Guntersville threatening to cross. The crew had seen enemy demonstrations at crossing the night before at Fort Deposit and Beard's Bluff three miles below Claysville. These were Wheeler's men doing their part to screen the Army's movement. Colonel Lyon, commander of Huntsville post and the railroad defenses from there to Stevenson, admitted that no one seemed to know Hood's intentions. Later in the day Granger reported that Hood was moving toward Somerville, and at 8:30 p.m. General Thomas duly notified General Sherman. Still believing Hood to be at Gadsden, Sherman sent out a strong reconnaissance force toward Gadsden to find out for sure.[36]

Granger also advised General Thomas that day that the river was so low at Guntersville that gunboats other than the *Stone River* could not come downstream. Hood's cavalry could probably ford the river if his army was near Guntersville, but he thought 2,000 infantry and a battery of artillery could prevent their crossing. The best ford on the river below Bridgeport was near there, he said. Shortly afterwards, he reported that nearly all of his men guarding block houses at the bridges along the Memphis and Charleston railroad and all along the north side of the river were prostrated with the ague, and he needed reinforcements badly. Granger had more reasons for concern than he knew. At about the same time, the Army of Tennessee was arriving and making camp at Somerville, just thirteen miles away from Decatur. He sent General Thomas a final message which he must have regretted later: "I see no reason to believe there is any enemy within a few days march of this place, and these are Roddey's men."[37] In the afternoon he took a train to Huntsville to see about the defenses of the railroad toward Stevenson, leaving his post commander Col. Charles C. Doolittle in charge of the fort.[38]

The garrison at Decatur on 25 October consisted of: the 102nd Ohio, commanded by Col. William Given; the Eighteenth Michigan under Maj. Edwin M. Hulburd; the Second Tennessee Cavalry, Lt. Col. W.F. Prosser (FIG. 8); the Tenth Indiana Cavalry, Maj. Thomas G. Williamson; a detachment of the Thirteenth Wisconsin, Capt. Edgar W. Blake; Battery A, First Tennessee Light Artillery, Capt. A.F. Beach; Battery F, First Ohio Artillery, Lt. Norval Osburn; and Battery D, Second Illinois Light Artillery, Capt. Charles Cooper. The total strength of the fort was about 1,750 men and 17 pieces of artillery. Of these units, the infantry regiments, which would man the rifle pits on the outer defense line and the fort parapet, were the weakest component. The Eighteenth Michigan had lost over 200 men and the 102nd Ohio 167 men captured when they attempted to relieve the fort at Athens during General Forrest's attack there on 23 September. Most of the 500 men of the Thirteenth Wisconsin were sick at their stations north of the river, and only 150 of the able-bodied had been able to reach Decatur the day before.[39]

The Second, Third and Fourth Tennessee Cavalry regiments made up the First Cavalry Brigade of the Fourth Cavalry Division, District of North Alabama. The Fourth Regiment had been detached earlier to General McCook in Georgia and been nearly destroyed. The Second and Third regiments and brigade headquarters had been at Decatur when General Forrest attacked Athens in September. Both regiments were sent to reinforce the defense of Athens and were surrounded by the Confederates. The Third was captured, but the Second escaped at night and returned to Decatur when they were confused with Forrest's Second Tennessee Cavalry, C.S.A. A few of the staff of the Third and eighteen to twenty of the First Brigade staff were at Decatur at the time and became part of Decatur's defense force.[40]

The men captured by Forrest at Athens had been sent to Castle Morgan, a prison camp at Cahaba near Selma. The following spring when they were exchanged, many of these men were sent to Memphis to board the steamer *Sultana* en route to Cairo, Illinois. Seven miles out of Memphis at 2:00 a.m., 27 April, the boat's boilers exploded, and it burned to the water line and sank. Some 1,585 men perished, including seventy of the 102nd Ohio, a number of the Third Tennesse Cavalry and most of the ninety-eight men of the Eighteenth Michigan who boarded. Wesley Lee of the 102nd Ohio managed to land on the east bank of the river and was the first survivor to reach Memphis with word of the disaster. It is said to be one of the world's greatest marine disaster, slightly surpassing the losses on the *Titanic*.[41]

CHAPTER FOUR

Testing Decatur Defenses

FOR THE TWO CORPS OF THE ARMY AT SOMERVILLE the bleak morning of Wednesday, 26 October, came too soon. After the soldiers had eaten their cold beef and corn pone and rolled up their blankets, they assembled in the camp areas and on the roads, and leading elements were on the march by 1:00 a.m., one regiment at a time. Brown's Division led Cheatham's Corps along the Cedar Plains Road toward the Danville Road, then north toward a campsite selected by an advance party of engineers two and a half miles south of Decatur. In Stewart's Corps, Loring's Division took the lead on the Decatur Road with the Thirty-fifth Alabama of Scott's Brigade as advance guard of the corps, and Companies B and D the advance of the regiment. Later in the day, after the other corps had left, Lee's Corps marched through Somerville and camped four miles beyond on the Decatur Road. At sunset the previous day Hood had ordered General Lee to follow Stewart's Corps to a point where a staff officer would meet him and direct him around Decatur. On the twenty-seventh he moved to McDaniel's Mill about thirteen miles southeast of Decatur. He took no part in the action at Decatur.[1]

General Hood and his staff left Somerville at 9:00 a.m. and rode to Mr. Scruggs' house on the Decatur Road four miles from the town. Here the administrative staff under Brig. Gen. Francis A. Shoup turned off toward the Danville Road. They reached the home of Gen. Jesse Winston Garth, two miles from Decatur, at 7:00 p.m. and established headquarters. Hood and his small military staff continued toward Decatur, passing through the ranks of the corps to General Stewart's headquarters near the front. Hood made his headquarters for the night at Mr. Scruggs' house. They reached the Garth home early on the 27th. General Garth was a prominent lawyer and a business and community leader who had served six terms as a state senator. After service in the War of 1812 he was a general in the state militia. At this time he was in his mid-seventies and had given up the law to farm his large plantation.[2]

About 2:00 p.m. near Decatur, General Stewart ordered his chief of artillery, Lt. Col. Samuel C. Williams, to place twelve guns to fire on the enemy's works there. Williams rode back to Myrick's Battalion not far from the head of the column and ordered Capt. J.J. Cowan and Capt. Pat Darden to place their batteries about 800 to 1,000 yards from the Union works when they reached the area. He told Capt. James Haskins to put one section of two rifled guns next to them on the left. From there he had to ride back the length of Walthal's Division to reach Trueheart's Battalion which was following the division. Capt. Edward C. Tarrant (FIG. 10) was nine miles from Decatur with the battalion when Williams found him and ordered him to place two rifled guns in line on the right of Cowan's Battery when he got to Decatur.[2a]

1st Lt. Albert T. Goodloe ftom Colbert County, Alabama tells of the dark, rainy march of the Thirty-fifth Alabama to

Flint River where his own Company D and Company B waded across, then stood guard while a pontoon bridge was laid for the following troops. When the bridge was finished, Companies B and D led the column toward Decatur. Three miles from town they were surprised to see a small force of Union cavalry approach from the direction of Decatur and begin skirmishing with the mounted officers and pickets leading the column. The regimental commander must have seen that the cavalry was moving into a potential trap. He ordered the regiment to deploy across the road and stay out of sight while the cavalry was at a distance. When the Union charge neared them they began firing from cover. At this, the attackers halted abruptly, wheeled about and retreated as fast as they could go. Most of the Confederates' rifles failed to fire due to the rain, saving the Union soldiers from a massacre, but the men enjoyed this small victory and made jokes about the Yankees' frantic departure. Some enemy saddles were emptied. The men of Company D were from Limestone County just across the river and may have been a little giddy at the prospect of crossing the river to home country. Union troops at Triana on the north bank of the river just east of Decatur reported hearing loud cheering among the Confederates that afternoon and night, probably from some of these men.[3]

The Union force attacking the Thirty-fifth was a company of about fifty men of the Tenth Indiana Cavalry under Lieutenant Snooks. They had been sent out a little before noon to reconnoiter on the Somerville Road. Their regiment had just been issued horses and equipped with cavalry sabers and carbines the day before, and this was their first scouting mission for Colonel Doolittle. Before this they had acted mostly as infantry. Lieutenant Snooks had sighted the mounted men at the head of the Confederate column, probably thinking it was a detachment of Roddey's cavalry. He approached them without hesitation and began skirmishing. When they fell back, he charged until he saw he was attacking a whole regiment of infantry forming in line of battle.[4]

A mile and a half from Decatur the Thirty-fifth Alabama came upon an enemy outpost and easily drove the pickets in toward the fort. At about this point the regiment was formed into a skirmish line and advanced to within 400 yards of the outer works of the fort where they were ordered to lie down and await orders. The rest of the brigade formed in line of battle behind them, partly in a skirt of woods to the right of the road.[5]

Shortly after this the artillery batteries began to arrive and deploy behind the line of the Thirty-fifth. Darden's battery opened fire, and other batteries formed on the line as they came up. Enemy return fire had the range on Tarrant's battery in his first location, causing him to move back fifty yards before joining the barrage. They kept up a continuous fire for about an hour when the enemy ceased firing. Without explanation they were ordered to retire.[5a]

The rest of Loring's Division turned to the right behind Scott's Brigade and went into line toward the river. As they came up later, Walthal's and French's divisions turned to the left off the Somerville Road. Maj. Gen. Samuel G. French's division was the last to arrive. It generally took sixty minutes for a division to deploy from a column into a line of battle, and it was dusk by the time they moved up to the line on the far left. They went into bivouac in a column of brigades, within easy reach of enemy artillery. (This formation in depth probably was used for spacing purposes. It was more vulnerable to cannon fire than a line.) General French sent Brig. Gen. Matthew D. Ector's brigade on to the Danville Road to guard it until Cheatham's Corps arrived. Ector was still absent after losing his left leg to a cannon shot at Atlanta, and his successor, Brig. Gen. William H. Young, had been wounded and captured at Alatoona. Col. Julius A. Andrews of the Twenty-third Texas Cavalry (Dismounted) was in command of the brigade.[6]

As Scott's Brigade fell into position on the right, three men of the Fifty-fifth Alabama must have looked across at the fort of Decatur with special feelings. What they had known as the center of the tree-shaded village was now a bare military post enclosed by an ugly dirt embankment and a muddy ditch. The town was hardly recognizable with most of the surrounding trees and houses leveled to clear fields of fire. Pvts. James L. Byrd and William Cox and Sgt. J.W. Gentry had come to enlist in the Fifty-fifth at Decatur in March 1862 when General Albert Sidney Johnston was gathering his army there to move toward Shiloh. Pvt. Thomas J. Butler had enlisted with them but was killed a few weeks later at Shiloh.[7]

Lt. Will McTeer of the Third Tennessee Cavalry was acting assistant adjutant of what was left of the First Cavalry Brigade staff that was headquartered in a small house at the fort. He and some others were eating dinner when the firing of Lieutenant Snooks cavalry and the pickets began to the east. He picked up a telescope and climbed to the roof of the house.

Lying flat on the peak of the roof he focused on the Confederates a mile away. They looked so close that he flinched whenever a rifle fired toward him. A heavy infantry skirmish line came out of the woods in perfect order, reaching a mile and a half southward from the river, he said.[7a]

When the Tenth Indiana Cavalry scouting party returned to the fort and excitedly reported their brush with a Rebel force of 400 men, Colonel Doolittle was not unduly disturbed. He wasn't expecting Hood to arrive for a day or two and thought the new cavalrymen were probably exaggerating a bit after a brush with some of Roddey's cavalry. Nevertheless, he put all units on alert. At noon the Twenty-ninth Michigan under Colonel Thomas Saylor arrived from Nashville by train and unloaded on the north bank of the river. As soon as they marched into the fort, Doolittle placed 100 of them in Fort No. 1 and the rest on the extreme left of the east parapet next to the river. They made up for the absence of 200 men of the Eighteenth Michigan and 102nd Ohio who had left early in the morning aboard the *Stone River* to scout up the river. The Twenty-ninth was a new regiment mustered into service at Saginaw on 3 October and had been stationed at Nashville since then.[8]

At 1:30 p.m. sentries from an outpost to the east hurried in to report the enemy advancing on the place, and Doolittle decided he had better ride out to see for himself what he was up against. A little way out, not far past the Somerville Road redoubt, he could see the gray column of Confederate infantry approaching. He halted just outside of enemy rifle range and watched. Fifty-four regiments of Stewart's Corps stretched back along the Somerville Road further than he could see. The eighteen regiments of Loring's Division were coming up the road in column formation, executing a right turn and forming into line toward the river with skirmishers out. He didn't linger to count regimental flags, but he no longer had the slightest doubt that this was a massive force of Hood's infantry and not a detachment of Roddey's cavalry. He galloped back to the fort to mobilize his defenses. He first sent Col. William Given with the part of the 102nd Ohio left in camp and the 150 men of the Thirteenth Wisconsin under Captain Edgar W. Blake to Fort No. 2. They were to cover the left flank and the six guns of Battery D, Second Illinois Light Artillery that were there under Lt. H.C. Barger.

Now moving hurriedly he found Capt. Myron W. Reed of the 18th Michigan and told him to take all of the regiment left in the fort — about 100 men were aboard the *Stone River* patrolling upstream — and proceed outside the fort. He didn't say where they were to go, so Captain Reed took his men out the Somerville Road to the right of the redoubt and occupied some rifle pits used for picket reserves. They stayed there until 8:00 p.m. when they were ordered back to the fort. With his infantry strength so low Doolittle ordered Captain Bullock, the base provost marshal, to get all off-duty bridge and guardhouse guards and bring them up to the parapet. Then he hurried to deploy his cavalry.[9]

Lieutenant Colonel Prosser of the Second Tennessee Cavalry had heard the firing from the pickets to the east and already guessed what was happening. Without waiting, he ordered Chief Bugler George House to sound "Boots and Saddles" and had formed the regiment into line by the time

Colonel Doolittle rode up to his quarters. On Doolittle's order he led his 150 cavalrymen eastward and deployed past the outer line of rifle pits that ran through the redoubt. A few minutes later Doolittle sent the 150 men of the Tenth Indiana Cavalry to form on the right of Prosser's line across the Somerville Road. The inexperienced cavalrymen moved out at a walk, and he had to ride out to Major Williamson and tell him they were supposed to trot.[10]

While he was dispatching the cavalry, Doolittle rushed Capt. Albert F. Beach with a section of two guns of Battery A, First Tennessee Light Artillery, to the redoubt. Artillery horses towed the guns through the sally port next to Fort No. 2 and out the Somerville Road. After the guns were unhitched, the horses and caissons were taken to a shallow swale behind a ridge in rear of the redoubt.[11]

Capt. Charles S. Cooper of the Second Illinois Light Artillery, who was post chief of artillery, ordered the signal gun in Fort No. 2 to fire a warning shot, then rode to Fort No. 1 and alerted Lt. Norval Osborn who was posted there with Battery F, First Ohio Artillery. Afterwards he accompanied the First Tennessee Artillery section to the redoubt. Before returning, he helped clear away the rubbish that had accumulated there so that the guns could be put in position.[12]

At first, Captain Beach's men in the redoubt couldn't see any enemy artillery, and they began firing at any group of Confederates in sight. Then suddenly the Confederate batteries that were partly obscured by trees zeroed in on them with a heavy volley. With a roaring sound the first shot passed over the redoubt and landed at the back of a regimental headquarters at the fort. The second shot hit a gabion that formed the embrasure on one of the guns at the redoubt. Howitzer shells overshot the redoubt and exploded among the horses in the rear. Eight of them were killed and three sets of harness destroyed, leaving no way for the artillery men to move the guns. Shortly afterward a solid cannon shot took off the heads of two caisson drivers, Privates Patrick Carroll and James Newberry, who were standing one behind the other. Volunteers almost argued over who would take their places. Other men nearby fell from their rearing horses, and the horses ran wildly along the line, creating a scene of confusion and destruction. Lt. Will McTeer, who had ridden to the redoubt with Captain Beach, was riding back to the caissons to send up ammunition when he was narrowly missed by a shell burst that killed an artillery horse behind the redoubt. "That was the only time while in service that I thought I would never see Mother again," he said. "Both shot and shell were plowing the ground until it appeared as if the earth was boiling like water while the roaring and wheeling of the deadly missiles rendered the air perfectly hideous."[13]

Enemy fire on the Union cavalry was severe as the rebels repeatedly attempted to advance with loud cheering and heavy volleys of musketry. To cover the front, Lieutenant Colonel Prosser had to extend his thin line to a mile and a quarter long. Because of the open and undulating terrain he could maneuver so as to conceal, then expose groups of his cavalry and give an exaggerated impression of his strength. Ignoring the heavy rifle fire, he rode back and forth along the line cheering and encouraging his men. A rifle shot hit and embedded in his saddle. Some of his men who were shot were lifted onto the fronts of their comrades' horses and taken to the rear. The cavalry was able to hold its position until infantry reinforcements arrived to occupy the line to the left of the redoubt.[14]

During the afternoon, eighteen-year-old Pvt. James M. Robertson, Prosser's orderly, and Sgt. Jesse Collins were killed. Capt. Aaron G. McReynolds, Sgt. Andrew C. Broady and Pvt. John A. Bryant of the Second Tennessee were mortally wounded. Captain McReynolds, who was from Maryville, Tennessee, and was highly regarded and popular among the men and officers of the regiment, was shot from his horse by a Confederate sharpshooter perched in a tree near the front. His men took a special satisfaction in shooting the Confederate out of the tree. McReynolds and Broady died the next day, and Private Bryant died on the thirtieth. Sgt. Rufus L. Mize, Pvt. Andrew Reaves and one other man were wounded. Several times Major Williamson of the Tenth Indiana sent word to Colonel Doolittle that he was afraid he couldn't maintain his position. Each time Doolittle replied that he must, and he did.[15]

With artillery fire from the redoubt playing into the lines of his division, General Loring pulled his main battle line back from the open country. The men took shelter in the woods, which were very thick there and extended some distance from the river. Twenty minutes later Colonel Doolittle ordered Col. Thomas Saylor's newly-arrived Twenty-ninth Michigan out to form on the left of the redoubt in a line of rifle pits running toward the river. They were the reinforcements the cavalry had been hoping for. Saylor at first sent out Lt. Col. E. Frank Eddy with 300 men of this regiment under a rapid and continuous fire from the Rebel artillery that was trying to silence the guns in the redoubt. Shortly afterwards, when the Confederates seemed to be preparing to advance, he sent out the rest of the regiment.[16]

As the engagement became more general, shot and shell were flying about the heads of the men in fort No. 2. Pvt. John F. Stone of the 102nd Ohio was wounded severely in the leg by a Confederate sharpshooter from about a half-mile away, and five other men of the 102nd were slightly wounded. Private Stone was later captured and was among those who perished when the steamer *Sultana* sank near Memphis in 1865. Since the gun crews in Fort No. 2 couldn't return fire without endangering the men in the redoubt, they had to watch in frustration while the two guns in the redoubt dueled the Confederate batteries.

At 3:00 p.m. Captain Cooper ordered a section of two guns to be placed in the east parapet between Fort No. 2 and the river as a precaution in case the enemy should advance on the works. (This probably was a part of Battery D, Second Illinois Artillery.) About that time Captain Beach came in from the redoubt to replenish his ammunition and reported he had several casualties and the men were very tired. Captain Cooper sent out a detachment of Battery F, First Ohio Artillery to relieve them, but Beach himself returned to the redoubt. By the end of the day Beach was told his guns had killed or wounded seventeen of the enemy, had killed ten horses and two mules and had blown up a caisson. Colonel Doolittle remained on the line of the outer defenses all afternoon and could attest that the redoubt was a hot place.[17]

Twice during the afternoon the Confederates tried to send
in flags of truce which Doolittle took to be demands for surrender. He ignored them when Hood continued to move his
men into position. About 4:00 p.m. he sent Lt. B.K. Davis
with the other section of Battery F, First Ohio Artillery from
Fort No. 1 out to the earthwork north of the redoubt. In a
short time the two smooth-bore 12-pounder Napoleon guns
of this section joined those in the redoubt to concentrate on
the guns of the enemy battery. (Colonel Doolittle reported
one Confederate battery with five guns, but Captain Beach
thought there were four guns partly masked (concealed)).
They believed the crossfire from their own four Napoleons
forced the enemy artillery to withdraw. About dark they saw a
Confederate battery moving toward the river.[18]

To the east, the Confederate batteries that had been
withdrawn from the line for about an hour were ordered to
move up again and resume firing. They fired intermittently
until dark, then fell back and went into camp. Late in the
afternoon Haskins' battery was ordered from the line and sent
down to the river to fire on the enemy's pontoon bridge, but
it was dark before they could deploy, and they were ordered
back to camp.[18a]

During the afternoon Haskins' two-gun section fired
eighty-six rounds. He had one man killed and one wounded.
Three horses were killed, and one of his gun carriages was
disabled. Captain Tarrant reported three men wounded: Pvt.
Mark Brooks of Taylorville, Alabama, had his arm shot off
at the shoulder; S.A. Spence was severely wounded in the left
thigh; and J.H. Brown was slightly wounded. In Darden's
battery two men were killed and one wounded, and one

limber was disabled by a solid shot. Cpl. "Tommie" Johnson of Cowan's Mississippi Battery was killed while preparing a fuse for a shell.[18b]

In Huntsville General Granger had been busy at his office all morning with messages and correspondence. After lunch he went to post headquarters and greeted Colonel Lyon with, "Colonel, I can not find out anything, and I have come here to find out what is going on."[19] Lyon had organized a number of citizen scouts who reported to him from both sides of the river, and some of them were tracking Hood's movements. He quietly told Granger that Hood was advancing on Decatur and would be there before night, to which Granger replied, "I do not believe it." As they talked, they heard the boom of distant cannons. Pricking up his ears, Granger asked, "What is that?" and Lyon replied, "It is Hood at Decatur." "It is impossible," Granger said.[20]

Shortly after this, at 3:00 p.m., the telegraph operator at Huntsville sent a message to the operator at Nashville, saying "Enemy attacking Decatur in full force."[21] At 3:25 p.m. General Granger relayed to General Thomas a message just received from Decatur in which Colonel Doolittle reported his cavalry's first encounter with the Rebels. Five minutes later Granger notified Thomas that he was leaving for Decatur by train in a few minutes with all the spare troops he could round up, but "I don't regard the attack on Decatur as serious, yet it can hardly be more than an advance of Hood's, if his forces are there at all"[22] His last transmission before leaving Huntsville relayed Colonel Doolittle's stark message, "The enemy are attacking us."[23] It was getting dark by the time Granger reached Decatur about 5:00 p.m. By then the severest fighting was over, and only a scattering of cannon and rifle fire continued.[24]

In the Confederate lines, most of the day's action had taken place in Loring's Division from the Somerville Road to the river where it had started. The brigades in this sector had mounted several attacks but, because of the vigorous defense, had not pressed them. The concentration of Union artillery on the Confederate batteries had made it a hot place, and the Thirty-fifth Alabama, in an exposed area near the guns, suffered heavily. They lost thirty-five men in killed and wounded during the siege, many of them this first day. An early casualty was Marion Harlan of Company C. While lying prone he was hit in the shoulder by a cannon ball which penetrated his body lengthwise, killing him instantly. William D. Pettus of Company D had his leg fractured by a musket ball. The wound developed gangrene and he was at death's door for a long time, but he survived with a serious permanent disability. He died in Huntsville in 1905. At Franklin, the Thirty-fifth was to lose 150 men killed and wounded, half of its effective force. The remnants of the regiment were among those to make it to the Carolinas after the campaign and surrender with General Johnston's army.[25]

About 3:00 p.m. Adjutant William E. Sykes of the Forty-third Mississippi of Adams' Brigade, Loring's Division, was severely wounded. When he fell, the Forty-third was in line of battle on land that formerly had been his father's plantation. He and a cousin, Capt. Edward T. Sykes, Adjutant of Jackson's Cavalry Division, had been born there. His brother, Lt. Col. Columbus Sykes of the Forty-third, went to his side and examined his wound, which appeared to be fatal. They carried him to a nearby house formerly owned by his father and laid him on an improvised couch. Lt. W.H. Berryhill of the Forty-third wrote to his wife that Adjutant Sykes was the best man in the regiment. As he lay dying he asked if he had made any enemies in the regiment. If so, he wished to see them to know the cause, Berryhill wrote.[26]

Pvt. J.M. Miller of the Twentieth Tennessee was in the battle line just to the left of the Forty-third Mississippi in Adams' Brigade. He noticed a grim result of the fort's cannon fire in that area: "I saw a man being borne on a litter with the top part of his head shot off by a cannon shot, leaving under jaw [sic] with chin whiskers an odd looking sight, his brains being spattered on his comrades."[27]

Nineteen-year-old Craig Hamilton Wilkinson of a Mississippi regiment, probably the Forty-Third, was wounded by a piece of shell. The same shell killed six horses and wounded a driver severely. Roger Sherman, also of the Forty-third Mississippi, had a close call when a bullet put a hole in his hat without leaving a scratch. He had been in this regiment continuously since he enlisted on 12 March 1862 and seemed proud that he had never been in the hospital. This was the closest he came to it during the war.[28]

Walthal's Division of Stewart's Corps did not complete its deployment to the left of Loring until late in the day. It was growing dark under heavy clouds, and cannon fire was in progress when Quarles' Brigade arrived. The First Alabama was sent forward immediately to form a picket line for the brigade. By the time they reached their position it was pitch dark. At 10:00 p.m. 2nd Lt. Daniel P. Smith (FIG. 15) and the men of Company F were ordered to advance and dig rifle pits

150 yards in front of the line. They did their best to move in a skirmish line, but it was difficult, since they couldn't see more than a few feet. About the time the rifle pits were completed a drenching rain poured down, filling the pits and converting the whole area into a marsh. When the rain stopped the men were so exhausted that as soon as they could bail out the pits, the ones not on watch lay down in the mud and slept.[29]

Cantey's Brigade came up on the left of Quarles to camp in line of battle, and the Twenty-ninth Alabama was sent out on picket duty just to the left of the First Alabama. Because they were in mud and water they dug their rifle pits mostly with tin cups and pans besides the few entrenching tools they had. At dawn the regiment was sent forward and had a brief skirmish with Union pickets that resulted in several casualties.[30]

Reynolds' Brigade moved behind the other two brigades of Walthal's Division and into line on their left. As the First Arkansas moved up to make camp, it was so dark that the squads couldn't see their file leaders. (Officially this was the Arkansas First Cavalry Regiment Mounted Rifles (Dismounted)). Cpl. William E. Bevens of Batesville, Arkansas, thought the Army had lost its way, and it would be impossible to finish the line of battle. He was standing and holding onto a sapling when a following column came up along a hog path, guessing its way. Each man was calling to the man in front to keep in contact. Near him a log lay across the path about knee-high, and he saw three different soldiers stumble into it and fall over into the mud. Each time, the man's gun went splashing into the man in front of him.

"There was cussin' all along the line," he recalled. Finally he and some others went out on the log to guide the men around it.[31]

The Fourth Arkansas of this brigade drew picket duty and was posted on the picket line next to the Twenty-ninth Alabama. Capt. John W. Lavender of Mt. Ida, Arkansas, described the area as low and seeming to be an old, dried-up pond. Before they got their rifle pits half dug, the rain had covered the ground so they couldn't continue digging. There was thunder and lightning, and the rain fell in torrents until it got one to two feet deep where they were. All they could do was stand there and take it. As he recalled it, "Now and then Some man would move about and fall in a hole we had Dug and got Thoroughly Ducked, then he would loose all his religion."[32] Before daylight the rain slackened and it turned colder. They had to stand in the water until eight or nine o'clock in the morning when they were relieved by the First Arkansas.

When they went back to camp, Captain Lavender's legs and feet "was all Bleeched white and Rinkled up as I have Seen women's hands from washing," he wrote. His rawhide moccasins had become so soft they wouldn't stay on his feet. He hung them on some sticks by the fire, and when they dried "they was as hard as a piece of sheet iron."[32] In his memoirs Captain Lavender said this night was one he would remember as long as he lived. He was captured at the battle of Nashville in December and spent the rest of the war imprisoned at Johnson's Island in Lake Erie. He was one of the twelve to fourteen men to return to Mt. Ida out of the 100 men of Company F who marched away in 1861.[33]

On the right of the Confederate line the transition to night watch was easier. The Twelfth Louisiana had occupied the forward picket line for Scott's Brigade all afternoon. At dark they were relieved by another regiment and withdrew to the woods where the rest of the brigade was already camped.[34]

When the day ended, the front line of Stewart's Corps lay deployed in a line of four-man rifle pits from the river east of town circling to a point south of the fort with an almost unbroken chain of camps several hundred yards to a mile behind this line. Cheatham's Corps began arriving at dusk and moved slowly into camps further around to the west across the Danville Road. They deployed in the late night hours and into the next day.[35]

Confederate prisoners taken during the engagement told their Union captors they had been promised their supper in Decatur on the twenty-sixth. The men in the camps and trenches had plenty of time to reflect on this irony during a long, miserable night. They had nothing to eat except a little beef and what bread some prudent ones had saved in their knapsacks or pockets. They had been on short rations of poor quality for nearly a month — three quarters of a pound of very coarse corn meal a day and a pound of freshly slaughtered beef, bones and all. The food was usually prepared in the wagon yards or the camps by men detailed from each company. Meat was boiled and issued daily, and bread was issued every three days. The bread was corn meal cooked as pones, browned but underdone, in Dutch ovens. By the time it reached the men, the ration had "shrunk in the pot" so much that the soldiers often finished their bread in a day or two and sometimes at one sitting. Many of them complained that the coarse corn meal gave them chronic diarrhea, but it was the quantity of the food, not its quality, that was bothering the soldiers at this time. Evidently the normal schedule for issuing rations had been upset by the routing of the wagon train so far to the south. Lieutenant Smith of the First Alabama said these conditions were to blame for the widespread private foraging which started there and became such a disciplinary problem for the army.[36]

Due to the limited transportation there were no tents, except for those of the medical department, regimental headquarters, brigade commissaries and quartermasters and general officers. Men and officers of the line had only what they could carry on their backs. Sputtering campfires that could be kept lit in the rain were about the only source of comfort to the men huddled under wet blankets. Some of them must have had oilcloths, a standard item of equipment, but probably not many. Infantrymen had a strong distaste for carrying extra weight. Mounted men and officers valued them highly. Dr. Urban G. Owen, surgeon of the Fourth Tennessee, wrote his wife from Tuscumbia, almost gleeful that he had two oil cloths and a new Yankee overcoat and was now ready for any kind of weather.[37]

Cpl. Angus McDermid, from the vicinity of the present town of Adel, Georgia, didn't even have a blanket and was barefooted. He said he had taken a blanket from a dead "Yanky" before they left Decatur, but he still had no shoes when he wrote to his family on 1 November, "Father I am plom bare footed. I haint got a sine of a shoe on my feet nor I don't no when I will hav."[38] McDermid was killed near Nashville on 7 December. Confederate dead and wounded

were left on the field, and during the night his body was totally stripped by the enemy. In the bitterly cold weather at
Nashville it was not uncommon for the dead of both sides to
be stripped of clothes and shoes by the enemy or, sometimes,
their own comrades.[39]

In the Federal lines at Decatur most of the men and all
the artillery were moved into the fort after dark. Indirect and
night firing by field artillery was considered a waste of time
and ammunition. One hundred men of the Twenty-ninth
Michigan were left in the rifle pits to the north of the Somerville Road redoubt. The men in the fort manned the ram-
parts or performed fatigue duty in shifts during the night.
The stormy weather was more bearable for them than for the
Confederates. They had plenty of food, and some had the
amenities of the garrison if they had the time for them —
tents and some log huts. Occasionally, in rainy weather some
of the men got to sleep on the porch of the hotel and a few
slept inside. Col. William Given who commanded the men
in Fort No. 2 said they worked the first two nights of the fight
in drenching rain without shelter and didn't have their clothes
off for four days and nights.[40]

About 10:00 p.m. the *Stone River* pulled up to the
boat landing with the 200 men of the 102nd Ohio and Eighteenth Michigan who had been scouting upstream. As they
were going ashore, a detachment of 100 men of the Seventy-
third Indiana under Capt. William C. Eaton was cautiously
crossing the pontoon bridge in rain and darkness. They had
come from Athens by train as reinforcements.[41]

One of General Granger's final duties that night was a personal one. At midnight he telegraphed his wife in Huntsville

to leave there on the first train and go north without stopping in Nashville. Somehow Mrs. W.D. Chadick picked up this bit of intelligence the next day, not long after Mrs. Granger received the message.[42]

Late this night Lt. G.H. Brewster and twenty men of the Eighteenth Michigan were sent out to some buildings outside the fort in the direction of the Somerville Road to prepare them for burning in case the enemy should drive in the pickets and attempt an assault. The next day they were sent back to occupy the buildings with orders to burn them and retreat inside the fort if the enemy advanced in force. Brewster and his men stayed there until 29 October.[43]

While Hood was already fretting for some word from General Forrest, General Taylor had just that day gotten around to sending Forrest the order to join Hood. The courtly language of his adjutant's message made it sound more like an invitation: "The Lieutenant General commanding directs, under instructions from General Beauregard, that as soon as you have accomplished the objects of your present movement your course will be directed toward Middle Tennessee, where you will put yourself in communications with General Hood."[44] The routine tone of this important directive wouldn't have caused any excitement or sudden action in Forrest's headquarters, and it was some days later before Forrest replied.

Early that day General Lee reported that he had left General Wheeler the previous midnight at Gadsden where his cavalry had been driven by an overwhelming force of Union cavalry and infantry. Wheeler had met the Fifteenth Corps of Maj. Gen. Oliver O. Howard's Army of the Tennessee

(Fifteenth and Seventeenth Corps). Sherman had sent them on reconnaissance to Gadsden on the twenty-fifth after General Thomas' report that Hood was near Decatur. They returned the next afternoon and reported that the enemy was gone, except for Wheeler's cavalry. General Howard's message to Sherman from Little River, Alabama, stated that all citizens told them the Confederates had moved north, but he didn't feel at all sure of this. "The Rebels have filled the mountains with scouts, and the sources of information are all barred up," he wrote.[45]

According to Maj. D.W. Sanders of General French's staff, Wheeler's outposts and pickets covered Sherman's front so thoroughly that it was impossible for him to obtain information from spies, deserters or inhabitants within Hood's lines, and Hood's movements were completely concealed from him. "The only instance in which Sherman's judgment was at fault and his headquarters without information of current events within his adversaries lines was when Hood broke camp at Gadsden and marched his army on the roads leading to Gunter's Ferry."[46] Hood was in front of Decatur before Sherman knew he had moved.

On learning that Hood had indeed left Gadsden, Sherman finally resolved that day to leave General Thomas to take care of the Confederates and to carry out his plan to march to the seacoast. He knew General Grant still believed the first priority should be to defeat Hood's army, but from this time forward he began preparations for his own campaign on the assumption that he could win Grant's approval. At 7:30 p.m. that night he ordered General Stanley to move his Fourth Corps the next day to reinforce General Thomas. When he notified Thomas of this at 8:00 p.m. he promised to go after Hood himself if Hood tried to cross at Guntersville. Otherwise, if Hood went to Decatur it would be up to Thomas to stop him. Possibly to reassure Thomas he added, "Beauregard may attempt Tennessee from the direction of Muscle Shoals, but when he finds me pushing for Macon, Milledgeville, etc., he will turn back."[47] An odd situation had developed where the opposing commanders would head in opposite directions, each expecting the other to follow him.[48]

CHAPTER FIVE

Vacillation, Fort Reinforced

THE AREA AROUND THE FORT AT DECATUR WAS oddly quiet in the early hours of Thursday, 27 October. A heavy fog that formed before daylight halted most of the gunfire and muffled the sounds of Cheatham's regiments arriving from the Danville Road. As the Confederate column groped its way along the west of the fort toward the river, patrols were sent out to guard their right flank and locate the Union lines. One group of these pickets was hailed in the fog by Union soldiers and replied, "Cheatham's men." When ordered to advance they walked squarely into the enemy soldiers and had to scramble back toward their lines, leaving behind two men who were shot. During the rest of the day Cheatham extended his line across the Moulton and Courtland Roads to the river west of the fort. His regiments established a long line of encampments on the Courtland Road.[1]

The fog and relative quietness must have had a calming effect on the soldiers. Men on both sides stood casually in the open within waving distance of each other, trusting that they wouldn't be shot at. The 102nd Ohio even brought out its band and started playing "Yankee Doodle." A Confederate band assembled and replied with "Dixie." Then it was "The Star Spangled Banner" answered with "Bonnie Blue Flag." This went on until some soldier shouted that he was going to start shooting, and everyone ducked behind the parapet or into a rifle pit, and the moment of peace was over. After the fog lifted, General Granger received reports from scouting parties east of the fort that the Confederates were throwing up an artillery breastwork upstream near the river. He called in Lt. Col. Jacob M. Thornburgh, former Commander of the Fourth Tennessee Cavalry and now his District Chief of Artillery, and told him to ride up the north bank of the river and see what the Rebels were doing.

Thornburgh assembled a small party of men, including Lieutenant Colonel Prosser and 1st Lt. Will McTeer and some men of the Second Tennessee Cavalry, and Captain Beach and Lt. John C. Kriedler of Beach's battery. They rode about a mile up the river where they could see the Confederates at work on an artillery emplacement. They rode up casually, not expecting any danger from small arms from across the wide river. Before they knew it they were ducking for cover under heavy and accurate rifle fire from the Confederate infantry line. It appeared to them that the Confederate earthworks were being made so that the guns in them would point straight out toward the gunboats in the river. Thornburgh selected positions for their own guns to counterfire at the enemy and they turned back hurriedly, still under fire from the infantry across the river.[2]

Based on Thornburgh's report, General Granger believed the Confederates would probably use this artillery to break his pontoon bridge and to fire on any gunboats engaged. He advised General Thomas of this development by message and said he was sending a rifled cannon across the river to enfilade the enemy line and that his gunboats were shelling them.

(Actually, only the *Stone River* was near at this time.) Heavy rifle fire was coming from a considerable part of the Confederate lines, he added, but he still believed the enemy force was Roddey's men and Hood's advance. He didn't see how Hood's main force could be much closer than Somerville, with the rain-swollen Flint River still to cross. He ventured to General Thomas that he wouldn't be surprised to learn Hood was bypaspassing Decatur through Oakville and Moulton to Tuscumbia.[3]

According to General Granger's after-action report, nothing of importance occurred on the twenty-seventh. Federal picket lines in rifle pits surrounded the fort, and Hood's men occupied a picket line several hundred yards from them, continuing to entrench their positions throughout the day. There was occasional artillery fire from the fort, but Granger's men observed no Confederate artillery. All of the Union artillery remained inside the fort. During the morning some of Cheatham's men drove in a small part of the Union picket line on the west side of the fort near the river, but in the afternoon fifty men of the Seventy-third Indiana under Lt. Alexander Wilson were sent out to reestablish the line. They deployed as skirmishers, moved forward at the double quick and drove the Confederates back to their line. Six men were wounded, and Pvt. Robert Flewellen of Company I was killed. Fire from the Confederate lines prevented them from removing his body, and it was left on the field. [4]

Captain James C. Wilson and seventy men of the Thirteenth Indiana Cavalry equipped as infantry arrived as reinforcements during the day, and at 4:00 p.m. about 500 men of the Fourteenth U.S. Colored Infantry under Col. Thomas

J. Morgan (FIG. 12) arrived from Chattanooga. The Fourteenth was organized at Gallatin, Tennessee by Colonel Morgan in November 1863 and since then had been stationed at Bridgeport, Dalton, Pulaski and Chattanooga. All of the officers were white. Most of them were soldiers from regiments in the Army of the Cumberland who had applied for commissions in the colored regiments. The men were enlisted from contraband camps, farms in Tennessee and surrounding states, and camp followers. It was the only regiment among the incoming reinforcements with any combat experience, having fought against Wheeler's cavalry at Dalton in August and against Forrest at Pulaski in September.[5]

Just before midnight on 25 October the men of the Fourteenth had been roused from their camp at Chattanooga and told to prepare for an immediate move. They plodded in lines through the rain to draw three days' rations and 100 rounds of ammunition, then were formed and hurried to the railroad station. The first men to board were loaded on three stock cars from which horses had just been unloaded. They had to stand up all night while the train headed westward. As they reached Stevenson at dawn and continued to the west, the soldiers in the cars had the first clue that they were headed for Decatur. On reaching the north bank of the river at Decatur on the afternoon of the twenty-seventh, they unloaded, and eight companies marched across the bridge into the fort. Two companies remained on the north bank and waited while Colonel Morgan and Lt. Col. Henry C. Corbin (FIG. 13) reported to General Granger.[6]

Behind Confederate lines, at a house near the camp of the Forty-third Mississippi, Adjutant William E. Sykes died at

10:00 a.m. Lt. Col. Columbus Sykes received permission to take his brother's body home for burial, and a small group of men gathered to help him load it on a wagon to begin the journey to Aberdeen, Mississippi. After completing this somber mission and taking leave at his home, Lieutenant Colonel Sykes didn't rejoin the army until after the Tennessee Campaign. On the night of his return to the regiment on 5 January 1865 at Marietta in Itawamba (now Prentiss) County, Mississippi, he and two other officers were killed at about 2:00 a.m. when a large, dead white oak tree fell across their campsite. His body was taken by ambulance to Aberdeen for burial.[7]

Lt. W.H. Berryhill of the Forty-third had written a letter to his wife, and asked Lieutenant Colonel Sykes, as he was leaving Decatur, to deliver it. In the letter Berryhill wrote that Jo Golding of the Forty-third had one of his arms cut off by a shell that day. It was cut with such force that his hand fell thirty yards behind him.[8]

In Walthal's Division southeast of town, skirmishers were sent forward at daylight. The First Alabama was assigned this duty for Quarles' Brigade. Finding the enemy in force they fell back to the picket line with the loss of one man in Company E mortally wounded. Soon afterwards, the regiment was relieved and rejoined the brigade to the rear. Lieutenant Smith of Company K said it rained at intervals all day, and, to add to the discomfort, no rations were issued except a little beef. There was no bread for two or three days. Smith was shot through the jaw later at Franklin and was in and out of hospitals until the war ended.[9]

In the early morning Pvt. Washington B. Crumpton of the Thirty-seventh Mississippi, Cantey's Brigade in Walthal's

Division, was put in charge of three men and sent forward to dig rifle pits close to the enemy. In the densest fog he said he had ever seen, they moved up with pick and shovels until they could distinctly hear the voices of Union soldiers. As they concentrated on digging, the fog lifted a bit, and when they looked up they saw some Union men in plain sight eating breakfast. They high-tailed it toward some woods a mile away. They were halfway there before they were sighted, and after that there must have been a thousand rifle shots fired at them, he said, but no one was hit. Crumpton thought that whoever gave the order for them should have been in an insane asylum or prison, but the Union defenders were equally misguided. They had no sentinels or pickets out and could have been captured with a regiment or two.[9a]

Maj. Gen. John C. Brown's division of Cheatham's Corps was camped in an open field nearly a mile wide directly in front of the southern point of the fort and near a small cemetery. Late in the afternoon W.J. Worsham, regimental musician and rifleman of the Nineteenth Tennessee of Gist's Brigade, went out with a few other men to a vedette post just in front of the fort. The fort looked to him no more than 400 yards away across an open field. Occasionally a cannon shot would pass over them. As they started back to their lines, a shot aimed at them from the fort hit the ground about 100 yards behind, glancing and hitting the ground every forty yards or so. It passed about ten feet to their right and went on into the woods. One of Worsham's recollections of this period was that the Fifteenth Mississippi of Loring's Division was noted for having six brothers in its ranks. All six of them were killed later in the battle of Franklin.[10]

From their camp in Brown's Division area, Pvt. Isaac W. Shannon of the Ninth Tennessee of Maney's Brigade, along with Maj. Mat Pilcher and Lt. John M. Ozanne and the rest of Company E, moved a mile forward to a hill in front of Decatur and opened fire on the enemy picket posts. One after another the picket posts returned their fire until the air was buzzing with minie balls. Private Shannon took cover behind a large oak stump that seemed to shrink as the bullets came closer and began to hit the stump. Bushes and limbs were falling, and dirt was flying everywhere. As he saw it, it was inadvisable to stay there in the open. At the time Major Pilcher gave the order to retreat, Lieutenant Ozanne was up in a tall water oak tree he had climbed at the foot of the hill to observe the enemy. He hadn't been there long when a three-inch rifled cannon fired at him from the fort and on the first shot hit the tree just below his feet, knocking out a "slab of timber big enough for a rail." "I've seen enough," he said, and scrambled down and ran back through a marsh. The next shot hit just behind him and splashed mud and water all over him.[11]

Except for two short sorties the artillery in Stewart's Corps spent the day in camp. Captain Darden kept his four teams of horses harnessed and hitched to the guns ready to move on short notice but was not called on. Haskins' battery was ordered to move its two rifled guns to the riverbank, but before reaching there was ordered to return. In mid-afternoon Guibor's battery was ordered to the riverbank to fire on enemy gunboats. They moved four miles upstream, and at about 4:00 p.m. opened fire on a boat. After firing fourteen rounds of solid shot they were ordered back to camp. They had no casualties.[11a]

Most of the Confederate regiments were moved to their right during the day as Hood adjusted his line to take in Cheatham's Corps and move closer to the riverbank east of the fort. Each brigade detailed one regiment to man a picket line of rifle pits about 400 yards in front of the main line. About 150 yards in front of the picket line they placed a series of vedette posts in rifle pits ten to fifteen yards apart. Some of these vedette posts were only 100 to 200 yards from enemy vedette posts. In the afternoon French's Division of Stewart's Corps was ordered to move left to the west of the Danville Road. They went into line at this new position not far in front of General Garth's home at sunset. On orders from General French three regiments moved forward to the picket line and relieved regiments of Brown's Division, then advanced and drove in the Federal pickets. There was firing all around, but most of it was on Loring's line east of Decatur, as General French noted in his dairy.[12]

After their last meeting at Gadsden, General Beauregard had expected Hood to cross the Tennessee River at Guntersville. While the Army marched away in that direction, Beauregard remained at Gadsden to prepare orders and correspondence, and Hood neglected to tell him of his change of direction to Decatur. On the twenty-fourth, as he was riding to join Hood, Beauregard was nearly to Guntersville when he heard of the change. He was astounded, but there was nothing he could do about it except to turn and follow with his small staff of eleven officers and men. They arrived at Somerville in mid-afternoon on the twenty-sixth and spent the night there while waiting for word on the location of Hood's headquarters.[13]

When he found Hood at Decatur on the twenty-seventh, Beauregard must have been steaming. If his language showed general-to-general restraint, there was no mistaking the reprimand he gave Hood. He "pointedly cautioned" Hood against the irregularity of his action. He "openly expressed his regret" that Hood had gone so far downstream to cross the river, since it would add almost 100 miles to the march to Stevenson and give Sherman and Thomas more time to prepare for a defense. He also told Hood he should have attacked Decatur by an all-out assault at dawn on the twenty-seventh rather than investing it, as Hood appeared to be doing, since the enemy was now prepared to resist.[14]

General Beauregard made his quarters at General Garth's home where Hood was staying, and for a brief time this was the field headquarters of the Confederate Military Division of the West and of the Army of Tennessee. Here Hood got reports that day from his corps commanders and reconnaissance patrols indicating the fort was too strong to be assaulted. According to General Beauregard, he decided that afternoon to move further down the river to make a crossing halfway to Courtland where he thought there would be an easier passage. For the time being, he continued his investment tactics that were already in motion for the next day.[15]

That night a detachment of infantrymen continued working on an entrenchment for the Confederate artillery. The site, as described by General Granger, was on the riverbank 1500 yards east of the fort in an area protected by a belt of timber and some broken ground. The infantry regiment next to the emplacement dug rifle pits diagonally back to connect it with the main picket line to complete the encirclement of the fort.

Just behind the batteries was a mound resembling an Indian mound. An infantry unit dug a trench from the river back across the mound and for a short distance beyond from which to back up the end of the main line and the artillery.[16]

In the fort the Second Tennessee Cavalry was posted, dismounted, on the east parapet all day. Three privates of Company K, which was next to the river, decided they might be able to capture the Confederate artillery position if given the chance. Reluctant to ask permission to try this bold plan, they left ranks and slipped along the shore until they were close enough to begin taking shots at the men working on the gun emplacement. Confederate infantrymen nearby soon spotted them and let loose a hail of rifle-fire that wounded Privates R.L. Neuse and Andrew Reaves. The other man, Pvt. James Smiddy, ran back to the fort to report the incident, and a few men were sent to bring the wounded men back.[17]

General Granger had been anxiously following the progress of the artillery entrenchments all day, knowing that any guns there could easily command the pontoon bridge and any gunboats that might come to the assistance of the fort. When he learned that the Fourteenth U.S. Colored Infantry would be arriving that day he decided to go ahead with his plan to send some artillery to the north bank. He could use the Fourteenth to build an earthwork to provide cover for the guns. About 4:00 p.m. Colonel Morgan and Lieutenant Colonel Corbin reported to him the arrival of the Fourteenth, and he quickly told them what he wanted done before dark. Colonel Morgan sent Corbin back across the river with instructions to take the two companies, 100 men, on the north bank and start work on an artillery emplacement upstream.

Lieutenant Colonel Thornburgh would go with them and
point out the location he had selected earlier that day.[18]

After they left, Granger told Captain Beach to get ready
to take a section of the First Tennessee Light Artillery across
the river after dark and move up to the earthwork site.
After Wednesday's battle, Beach had only enough horses and
harness left for the two guns. His orders were to cooperate
with the gunboats in silencing any enemy guns placed in the
earthwork. The now-weary Lieutenant Colonel Thornburgh
would cross the river again with him and help with the
placement of the guns. Beach and his men were busy from
then until dark wrapping the wheels and traces of his guns
with rubber and rags to muffle their noise and avoid discov-
ery. They painted the two brass James rifles black, chalked
the sights, and were ready by dusk. Sometime after dark they
gingerly led the artillery horses across the bridge by the light
of lanterns and moved up to where the gun emplacements
were being prepared.[19]

Lieutenant Colonel Corbin and his men had moved
upstream about a mile from the railroad while it was still daylight. Beginning after dark they worked hard all that night,
getting the guns in position just before sunrise on the twenty-
eighth. The infantrymen then deployed in a skirmish line
along the riverbank on each side of the guns.[20]

During the night the men in the fort watched uneasily
as more than a thousand Confederate campfires flickered at
them from every direction. If General Granger still had doubts
that he was facing a heavy enemy force, they disappeared at
nightfall. At 2:00 a.m. the other section of Battery A, First
Tennessee Light Artillery under Lt. James Tobin, and fifty

more men of the Seventy-third Indiana under Lt. Col. Alfred B. Wade, arrived from Athens and crossed the bridge in the dark. At the same time, Lt. Col. Harvey J. Espy and the Sixty-eighth Indiana Infantry were unloading from a train from Chattanooga. Espy reported to headquarters in the fort and was assigned to a position on the right of post headquarters. At 5:00 a.m. he sent Capt. Giles E. White with 100 men to occupy a skirmish line extending across the railroad and the Courtland Road. For a few hours, traffic across the bridge had been almost continuous. By now the strength of the garrison totaled 3,000 men, and the fort was becoming crowded with tents, horses, men and equipment. Inspectors claimed the breast-high parapet fully protected men in the rear, but the soldiers couldn't help hunkering down as they moved around on their duties.[21]

Earlier that day, General Wheeler's cavalry scouts detected the movement of Sherman's 4th Corps from Gaylesville toward Chattanooga, and Wheeler promptly dispatched a courier to General Hood with this intelligence. In Nashville, General Thomas decided during the day to move this corps on to Pulaski, Tennessee, where he would concentrate whatever reinforcements he could get into a forward defensive force. From there he could meet a direct advance of Hood's army from Decatur or move east or west to cover approaches by Stevenson or Florence. He was well aware that he couldn't prevent Hood from crossing the Tennessee and that he needed reinforcements to successfully defend the line west of Stevenson. With a hint of desperation he asked General Sherman about the troops from Missouri that he had been continually promised. If he could get them in four days, he said, he would position them at Eastport, Mississippi, to threaten Hood's left flank, which he thought would keep him from invading Tennessee. That night he telegraphed General Granger to be especially careful to prevent any attempt of the enemy to attack him in the early morning hours.[22]

At Gaylesville, General Sherman was impatient to move back toward Atlanta and prepare for his march to the coast, if General Grant approved it, but he decided to wait a few days to hear what headway Hood would make at Decatur. As he wrote to General Halleck "[I] may yet return to Tennessee; but it would be a great pity to take a step backward. I think it would be better to let [Hood] ravage the state of Tennessee, provided he does not gobble up too many of our troops."[23]

FIGURE 1   77

GEN. JOHN B. HOOD
C.S. Army Commanding,
Army of Tennessee

BRIG. GEN. ROBERT S. GRANGER, U.S.A.
Commander, District of North Alabama
(headquartered at Decatur),
Army of the Cumberland

FIGURE 3   79

GUNBOAT *GENERAL SHERMAN*
Guns on bow not shown.

U.S. NAVAL HISTORICAL CENTER

MAJ. GEN. BENJAMIN F. CHEATHAM, C.S.A.
Commander, I Corps, Army of Tennessee

NATIONAL ARCHIVES

FIGURE 5   81

LT. GEN. ALEXANDER P. STEWART, C.S.A.
Commander, III Corps, Army of Tennessee

MAJ. GEN. SAMUEL G. FRENCH, C.S.A.
Division Commander, Stewart's Corps, Army of Tennessee

FIGURE 7 83

MAJ. GEN. WILLIAM W. LORING, C.S.A.
Division Commander, Stewart's Corps,
Army of Tennessee

LT. COL. W.F. PROSSER, U.S.A.
Commander, Second Tennessee Cavalry,
garrisoned at Decatur

U.S. ARMY MILITARY HISTORY INSTITUTE

FIGURE 9   85

COL. CHARLES C. DOOLITTLE, U.S.A.
Post Commander, Union Garrison at Decatur

CAPT. EDWARD C. TARRANT, C.S.A.
Alabama Battery, Trueheart's Battallion,
Stewart's Artillery Corps

FIGURE 11   87

SGT. JOEL D. MURPHREE, C.S.A.
Quartermaster Sergeant, Fifty-seventh Alabama,
Scott's Brigade, Loring's Division, Stewart's Corps

DEPARTMENT OF ARCHIVES AND HISTORY, STATE OF ALABAMA

COL. THOMAS J. MORGAN, U.S.A.
Commander, Fourteenth Colored Infantry

MASSACHUSETTS COMMANDERY, MILITARY ORDER OF THE
LOYAL LEGION, AND U.S. ARMY MILITARY HISTORY INSTITUTE

FIGURE 13   89

LT. COL. HENRY C. CORBIN, U.S.A.
Fourteenth Colored Infantry

NATIONAL ARCHIVES

PVT. R.H. NATIONS, C.S.A.
Twelfth Louisiana, Scott's Brigade, Loring's Division,
Stewart's Corps

GEORGIA DEPARTMENT OF ARCHIVES AND HISTORY

FIGURE 15   91

LT. DANIEL P. SMITH, C.S.A.
Company F, First Alabama

PONTOON BRIDGE AT DECATUR

CHAPTER SIX

Counterattack Stalls Demonstration

A S THE CLOUDS CLEARED AWAY THURSDAY NIGHT the weather turned colder. In the early hours of Friday the twenty-eighth a heavy frost formed, and fog blanketed the area. At 3:00 a.m. Confederate soldiers were roused shivering from their blankets to begin a movement all along the line to tighten the siege around the fort. Elements of both of Hood's corps charged enemy picket lines and drove them in toward the fort. In the dark they took possession of the ravine which ran around the town 800 yards out and began entrenching their positions. By dawn their rifle pits extended across the southern front and from the railroad diagonally across the western front to the river. General Granger estimated the enemy force in line on the west of the fort as three brigades of infantry and sharpshooters.[1]

From the Moulton Road to the river most of the new Confederate line was about 500 yards from the fort except for a section from Fort No. 1 to the river. In this area a detachment of men from each brigade of Bate's Division under Maj. Theodore D. Caswell of the Fourth Georgia Sharpshooter Battalion had been ordered to move forward as near as possible to the fort. During the night they drove in the enemy pickets and dug rifle pits in some places to within 200 to 300 yards of the parapet, some of them on the same plateau. A detachment of Cleburne's Division between their left and the river moved up on the same line.[2]

After sunup the fog began to dissipate under a clear sky. Soldiers in the fort peering over the parapet could see enemy infantry lines in all directions covering them from almost every angle. To one gun crew in Fort No. 1 the danger of this situation was made painfully apparent soon after daylight. A Confederate rifleman was in a "gopher hole" directly in line with the embrasure of a heavy cannon. Every time the crew tried to load or aim the gun the rifleman would shoot at them through the opening. For some time the gun was made harmless by this one man. Finally the gun crew was able to load and aim the gun at the mound of dirt in front of the Confederate soldier while he was reloading. As he was coming up to fire again, one cannon shot and killed him and buried him in the hole.[3]

From his headquarters General Granger saw that the Confederate riflemen on the far right of the fort were in a position where they could, if he didn't do something, partially enfilade Fort No. 1 and fire into the rear of Fort No. 2 to immobilize the guns there. Hurriedly he organized a small group of about fifty men of the 18th Michigan, the 102nd Ohio and the 13th Wisconsin, most of them clerks and orderlies from district headquarters. He put Captain William C. Moore of the 18th Michigan in command of this small force and ordered him to attack the enemy in the closest line of rifle pits on the right. To support the charge he instructed the artillery on the west of the works in Fort No. 1 to load with canister (a can or bag of marble-size pellets having an effect like buckshot) and to begin firing on the Rebels as soon as Captain Moore's men made their appearance. Fort No. 2 was ordered to fire shells on the southern end of these rifle pits at the same time, and the men on the breastworks were told to pour in a rapid fire of musketry along the enemy line. Then Granger collected another force of 500 men under Lieutenant Colonel Thornburgh to move out a sally port next to Fort No. 1 and support the attacking party as soon as the attack was discovered by the enemy.[4]

When everything was ready, shortly before 8:00 a.m., Captain Moore and his men moved downstream along the river under cover of the high bank until they reached a cane brake on the edge of the bank about a thousand yards from the fort. After a brief halt they filed carefully up the bank through the cane to the far edge of the brake, then on hands and knees toward the rear of the Confederate rifle pits. With a yell that was picked up by the men on the parapet, they charged the left end and rear of the enemy line. The startled Confederates quickly realized they were outflanked and began to abandon their trenches, only to be met by the artillery and rifle fire from the fort. One of the fort's guns was a heavy mortar with a bore about a foot in diameter and it fired with a report that seemed to shake the earth. Every time it fired the retreating Confederate soldiers could be seen to jump.[5]

General Granger's headquarters were in the Hinds-McEntire home on the river a little west of Fort No. 1. The two-story brick structure had a flat lookout roof enclosed by a wooden railing, making it a perfect place for observation. Lieutenant Colonel Thornburgh and Lieutenant McTeer, who were at headquarters at the time, took the opportunity to climb to the roof and watch as the attack developed. They could see the glistening bayonets of the attacking party as it moved through the cane but couldn't see the men. When the charge began, Thornburgh became excited, jumped up and fired down at the enemy soldiers with the rifle of a sentinel posted there. After this they hurried down to Fort No. 1 where Thornburgh halted the artillery fire and ordered his force out to the left of the closest Confederate trenches to hold the rest of the enemy line in position.[6]

On Thornburgh's order Lt. Col. Alfred B. Wade moved the Seventy-third Indiana out the sally port next to Fort No. 2 to draw the enemy's fire, then deployed by companies. Capt. Myron W. Reed and 150 men of the Eighteenth Michigan reported to him there and were ordered to take position on the left of the Seventy-third near the junction of the Moulton and Courtland Roads. Brisk skirmishing began with some Confederates concealed along the railroad.[7]

After these two regiments had cleared the sally port, Lieutenant Colonel Thornburgh decided to take Captain Bird's company of the Second Tennessee Cavalry and ride out to draw the enemy fire away from the rest of the force. Lieutenant Colonel Prosser joined him, and they started toward the gate at Fort No. 2. Just as the two officers and three men got outside the gate, heavy rifle fire forced them back after they had circled a small area. Sgt. James McFall of the Second Tennessee was killed on this sortie. The rest of Bird's company remained in the fort due to the heavy rifle fire coming at them over the parapet. When it was over, Thornburgh admitted to Lieutenant McTeer that he had been excited and acted the damn fool in taking the cavalry out.[8]

A hundred men of the Sixty-eighth Indiana under Capt. Giles E. White had already been on picket in the area since 5:00 a.m. Their line extended 100 yards left of the railroad and 100 yards to the right of the Courtland Road. When the sortie developed, White sent out forty men on his right to cut off the retreat of the Confederates from that direction. They brought in a number of prisoners and small arms.[9]

In the confusion of their sideways retreat a number of Confederates were killed or wounded, while others threw down their rifles and ran toward the advancing column waving their hats in surrender. A total of 120 were captured, including five officers. A captain was left on the field mortally wounded, and a major was brought into the fort wounded in the stomach. He didn't realize his wound was serious until, unexpectedly, as they were hurrying into the fort, his intestines fell in front of him and entangled his feet. A rifle ball had cut across his front leaving a long slit in his abdomen. Doctor John A. Souers, surgeon of the First Cavalry Brigade, tended him carefully for the next twenty hours but he died the next day. Captain Moore's little band swept almost the entire length of this section of rifle pits before halting, their strength reduced by the men guarding prisoners. Under the protection of Lieutenant Colonel Thornburgh's detachments, they retreated and returned to the fort with casualties of only three men slightly wounded. They were back in the fort less than an hour after they started.[10]

As brief as it was, this successful sortie was important to General Granger because it gave his men some much-needed confidence, besides clearing the enemy from a threatening position. He lost no time in reporting his success to

General Thomas, who responded at 11:00 a.m. with rousing congratulations: "I believe you can whip Hood's whole army from what I have heard of Decatur .... Troops that can do what yours accomplished this morning can accomplish almost anything."[11] Granger was not so sure of this. At the time, he believed Hood's entire army, including Lee's Corps, was in his front and determined to have the fort.[12]

Not long after this skirmish, Col. William D. Mitchell, commander of Jackson's Brigade of Bate's Division, led a detachment of men who attacked and reoccupied the positions they had lost, taking eight to ten casualties in the process. After this, the Confederate left settled back into routine picketing but with considerably more attention toward the river. No doubt General Cleburne made sure his line extended all the way down to the riverbank.[13]

Three of Bate's regiments engaged in this action took a large share of the Confederate casualties. The Thirty-seventh Georgia Infantry of Tyler's Brigade was in the line of rifle pits overrun by the Union attack. They lost thirty-three men captured. In the Sixty-sixth Georgia of Jackson's Brigade twenty-four men and one officer were captured. 2nd Lt. M.B.F. Nelms was killed. Pvt. Charles H. Stephens was permanently disabled by a head wound from shellfire, and Pvt. John E. Hodges was shot in the thigh and had his leg amputated above the knee. The Sixty-sixth took part later in recovering the area lost in the Union attack. The Twentieth Tennessee of Tyler's Brigade had about thirty men captured.[14]

The Thirtieth Georgia of Jackson's Brigade had no men captured, but took several casualties. Lt. Oscar L. Berry and Pvt. David Golightly were killed. 5th Sgt. James M.

Thompson was wounded in the left leg that had to be amputated above the knee, and he was discharged for disability. 2nd Lt. Elias Adams was wounded and permanently disabled. Three company commanders were wounded. Captains J.O. Redwine and Felix L. Walthal returned to duty soon afterwards, but Capt. Raleigh Hightower was sent home to Henry County, Georgia, to recuperate. He returned to duty in time to be wounded at Franklin and again at Murfreesboro. The captured men were sent to Camp Douglas near Columbus, Ohio, where fourteen died of disease or the wounds they had received.[15]

At 10:00 a.m. the Third Michigan Infantry under Col. Moses B. Houghton arrived in the fort from Nashville, giving another boost to the morale of the besieged men. This regiment, reorganized from new men and a few veterans, was mustered in on 15 October at Grand Rapids and left there on the twentieth directly for Decatur. It was assigned to the east parapet of the works where during the afternoon Pvt. Francis Lucas was mortally wounded. Private Lucas had the sad distinction of being the only enlisted man in the reorganized regiment to die from battle action until the war ended. One officer was killed later. Their record for escaping serious losses came to an abrupt end not long afterwards. In July 1865 the regiment was shipped to Texas, and within a short time after landing at Indianola en route to San Antonio, 156 men died of disease blamed on bad water and the heat, mostly at nearby Green Lake where they camped until September.[16]

The previous afternoon Lieutenant Colonel Williams of Stewart's Corps was ordered to place as many guns as possible on the river before daylight the next morning to fire on the pontoon bridge. At 4:00 a.m. on Friday he ordered Haskins', Tarrant's and Darden's batteries to move into position in the earthworks being prepared on the river. He led Tarrant down to the riverbank in the dark. By dawn he had placed Tarrant's battery in the center position with Haskins on his left, each with two rifled guns, and Darden on their right with four Napoleon guns. Darden was to fire at gunboats that might appear. Just as day was breaking Williams discovered that the earthworks, which should have been completed by then, had hardly been started. He also discovered the enemy mounting a gun on the river opposite Darden and Tarrant that bore on them and on Haskins' flank. He ordered the batteries to get to work making the place as safe as possible before sunrise when it was light. At that time he saw another enemy gun preparing to fire directly in front of Haskins' guns with a flanking fire on Tarrant and Darden.

After sunrise Union sharpshooters started a brisk fire and made it impossible for the Confederate artillerymen to complete the fortification or fire their guns. Williams ordered the batteries not to open fire until they could be protected by the infantry, then he left to find a brigade commander or the division commander to request sharpshooters to form a line facing the enemy across the river. When he returned at noon no infantry had appeared, although Brigadier General Featherston told him two companies had been directed to the site. About that time he was called away to take Kolb's and Guibor's batteries upstream to fire on the gunboats.[16a]

Capt. Henry Romeyn commanded Company B of the Fourteenth U.S. Colored Infantry that had spent the night digging entrenchments on the north bank for Captain Beach's two guns. As soon as the fog lifted enough to see across the river that morning, he climbed a tall tree to observe the Confederate artillery position. He could see that men were still working on the emplacements for their shore batteries and that they were not completed. More importantly there was no infantry support line for the guns as far as he could tell. He came down and reported this to Lieutenant Colonel Corbin. They concluded that the enemy batteries could be successfully assaulted and possibly captured by an infantry force. Corbin sent a scribbled plan for an attack and Romeyn's sketch of the terrain by a courier to Colonel Morgan.[17]

As visibility permitted, Captain Beach's two guns and the infantry on the shore opened fire on the Confederate batteries. From their position a little way downstream the Union guns and infantry could fire at the shore batteries from a slight angle, partially enfilading them. One gun could fire almost directly down the Confederate picket line. Lieutenant Colonel Corbin, commander of the Union detachment, reported killing and wounding a number of Confederates and dismounting a caisson with their fire, and some of his own men were also wounded. A private in Company B who had taken a position in a tree as a sharpshooter had his right arm broken by a rifle ball. Captain Romeyn told him he had better come down and go to a surgeon, but the soldier said, "Oh no, Captain, I can fire with my left arm," and he stayed at his position.[18]

At 9:00 a.m. Maj. Nicholas J. Vail was sent to relieve Corbin who returned to the fort. Major Vail continued the artillery and rifle fire against the Confederate batteries. One cannon shot exploded an ammunition chest of an enemy battery and killed and wounded some of the gun crew. Other shots tore up parts of the earthwork. All this time the infantry sharpshooters kept up a harassing fire on the embattled Confederate artillerymen, killing and wounding several of them. Confederate infantry near the shore kept up an almost constant return fire.[19]

At 9:30 Cowan's battery was ordered to join the other Confederate batteries on the riverbank. They took a position a little upstream from the shore batteries' works, where they would be masked by trees along the shore. They didn't take fire from the Union guns during the morning, possibly because of their position.[19a]

About mid-morning Captain Romeyn climbed back into the tree he was using for observation to see what damage had been done to the enemy position. This time he noticed that a Confederate infantry force that he judged to be a brigade was moving into a ravine on the river bank a little way upstream from the artillery. This put a decidedly different light on the plan they had submitted earlier. It would be nearly suicidal to attack an enemy force of this size, and a regimental assault now seemed out of the question. Major Vail quickly wrote a note to this effect to Colonel Morgan and gave it to a mounted orderly to deliver.[20]

Despite their numerical superiority in guns, the Confederate artillery batteries were almost completely ineffective. Union sharpshooters across the river kept them from completing any protective barrier. Rifle fire from the forward Union infantry line, which ran north from the Somerville redoubt on their left rear, was hitting the ground around them, and occasional cannon fire from the fort was playing into their rear. The only protection they had was the thin Confederate picket line on their left. All they could do was seek cover and wait for infantry support. Captain Darden sent two written requests for sharpshooters to cover them, but there was no response until much later.[20a]

General Granger was still elated over the victory in the attack on the west of the fort when Colonel Morgan met with him in mid-morning. Morgan showed him Lieutenant Colonel Corbin's plan for assaulting the Confederate shore batteries and volunteered the Fourteenth U.S. Colored regiment for the task, to which Granger quickly agreed. He called in Colonel Doolittle, and they carefully went over the details and timing of the support that would be needed for the attack. He and Doolittle spent the rest of the morning lining up a network of covering forces. They decided to send Lt. Col. Alfred B. Wade's Seventy-third Indiana Infantry to the line of rifle pits north of the Somerville Road redoubt to cover the Fourteenth as it moved into position on their left to launch the charge. Granger also told Doolittle to place a gun in the redoubt and one in the earthwork north of it. At 10:30 a.m. Granger sent word by courier to Major Vail to halt his rifle fire from the north bank when the infantry charge began and to concentrate Captain Beach's artillery fire on the Confederate guns. Then he ordered Captain Naylor to run the enemy batteries with the *Stone River* and get into position upstream to fire on their right flank with his long-range guns. They were to fire on cue from Beach's guns on the north bank of the river.[21]

The plan of attack for the Fourteenth U.S. Colored was brutally simple: Colonel Morgan and his 355 men were to move out next to the line of rifle pits where the Seventy-third Indiana would be deployed and charge across a half-mile of open ground. They would cross intervening Confederate rifle pits and bring off or spike the entrenched cannon. A little before noon Colonel Morgan assembled the regiment on the street in front of the McCartney Hotel. As he explained the mission to his men, the enemy batteries were to be charged and taken even if only ten men survived to take them. They were to allow no prisoners to be massacred but to give quarter to those who asked for it. The men showed no undue excitement or fear and seemed anxious to get on with the attack. Morgan then had them take off their knapsacks and other excess equipment and keep only their rifles, ammunition and a canteen of water. The excess equipment was stacked under a few guards by the street. Rat-tail files were distributed among the officers and some of the men in each company for spiking the cannons. They were told to drive a file into the fuse vent of a cannon and break off the outer part flush with the surface, then bend the inner part with a rod inserted through the muzzle. Lieutenant McTeer watched these preparations from the upper porch of the hotel and noticed that some of the officers were carrying hatchets for driving in the spikes or cutting the spokes of the cannon wheels.[22]

About noon Colonel Morgan led his eight companies in column out of the extreme east end of the fort at the river and marched parallel to the river to a point 780 yards from the enemy artillery battery. Here they halted, and the Colonel gave his final instructions. Two companies were designated as skirmishers to push forward rapidly while firing. They were instructed to assemble in the rear when the charge ended and afterward to retake their places in line. The other companies were to move in line of battle at "right shoulder shift" behind the skirmishers and were not to fire until the enemy works were taken. The company on the left was told to skirt the riverbank, and the others to guide them on. The regiment then turned toward the river and marched 150 yards under cover of the bank and up on the left of the Seventy-third Indiana's line of rifle pits. They halted, and the battle line was formed.[23]

Minutes before this, on the north bank of the river Major Vail and Captain Romeyn were stunned when the courier they had sent to cancel the assault rode up to them. He couldn't find Colonel Morgan and hadn't delivered the note, he told them. Romeyn told the man to dismount from his horse, then vaulted into the saddle and galloped to the bridgehead. He had to slow to a walk to cross the bridge, and when halfway across he looked to his left and saw the men of the regiment filing down the riverbank to use it as a screen while moving to the starting point for the charge. It was too late to stop them, but he went on to find General Granger and explain the situation. Granger quickly scribbled an order to Colonel Morgan to withdraw immediately and gave it to Romeyn to deliver.[24]

About this time, two companies of the Fourteenth were spreading out to the front in a skirmish line ready to advance. The remaining six companies formed in line of battle about 150 yards long. The companies in two ranks lined up side-by-side with a three-yard interval between companies. Company commanders stood on the right of the front rank of their companies. Lieutenant Colonel Corbin, junior

company officers and most of the noncommissioned officers lined up behind the regiment as "file closers" to prevent
men from dropping behind. They dressed ranks a final time
as the regimental flag was unfurled. The colonel moved to
front and center, and led the battle line forward. As they
reached the crest of a ridge they began to receive enemy fire.
Colonel Morgan ordered "Forward, double quick," and the
charge began.[25]

In the Confederate line facing the attackers, Featherston's
Brigade was nearest the river and connected on the right to the
shore batteries, with Adams' Brigade on its left and Scott's
Brigade extending to the Somerville Road. A few companies
manned a thin picket line in front of each brigade. The remaining companies of the picketing regiments formed a
reserve a few hundred yards to the rear, and regiments not on
picket duty were behind them in the camp area. A small force
occupied the trench over the Indian mound behind the batteries. As the Fourteenth appeared in full view, it immediately
drew the fire of the Confederate pickets in front of Featherston's and Adams' Brigades. By the time these men realized
they were being charged, the attackers were closing in and it
was too late to do anything about it.

They were forced to retreat, leaving the batteries unpro-
tected. The unarmed artillerymen had to abandon their guns
and leave their casualties behind as the men of the charging
infantry swarmed into the nearest emplacement and began
spiking cannons. The Confederates in the trench over the
mound saw that they were being attacked by Negroes and
wouldn't retreat or surrender. They were attacked with bayonets and finally had to give way, but when help arrived they

returned to the fight. The attackers had spiked two guns and were preparing another to be towed away when part of the Thirty-first Mississippi moved toward the emplacement from the far side. This probably was the force Captain Romeyn had seen moving into position upstream of the batteries and thought was a brigade. After some heavy hand-to-hand fighting the Fourteenth was ordered to withdraw by Colonel Morgan, who had just received General Granger's message. During the fighting in the gun positions the *Stone River* moved upstream and waited to the east of the Confederate batteries.[26]

The Confederates recovered quickly. As the Fourteenth fell back, the Thirty-first Mississippi advanced along the riverbank toward their rear, almost cutting them off. Many of the men retreating along the shore were shot by the Mississippians following along the bank above them. At the same time, the picket reserves of Loring's three brigades moved forward toward the attacking party, advancing some distance before they were stopped by heavy rifle fire from the Seventy-third Indiana. The Fourteenth barely made it back to the ravine where they had started twenty minutes before with the Thirty-first Mississippi in hot pursuit, threatening to roll up the flank of the Seventy-third in the rifle pits there. "A fleet foot saved the regiment," as Colonel Morgan wrote in his report.[26a] On the retreat, Captain A.H. Rolph killed a Confederate with his sword, and a soldier dispatched another with his rifle butt. Capt. C.W. Baker brought in a prisoner, and they released two wounded Confederates they had captured.[27]

The Fourteenth lost two men killed, fifty-two wounded and two missing in the attack. 1st Lt. George W. Apthorpe was one of the mortally wounded, and he may have been the man Lieutenant McTeer, who had watched the charge from beginning to end, saw being brought in on a stretcher. When the Fourteenth returned to the fort, a large, fine-looking lieutenant was carried right under where he was standing on the upper porch of the hotel. A rifle ball had passed through the man's temple leaving his eyeballs hanging out on his cheeks. His arms were broken and it appeared his legs were torn up, but he was still struggling against two men who were holding him down on a stretcher. He died later in the day. Three of their wounded and one man killed were left on the field. Two of the wounded escaped later and returned to the fort under covering fire from pickets of the Seventy-third Indiana. The other wounded man, rifle still in hand, and the dead soldier were recovered the next morning. Only two men left their arms on the field. Sergeant Samuel King brought in two enemy rifles. Colonel Morgan estimated they killed or wounded forty Confederates and captured fourteen. A number of the Confederate casualties were from the Thirty-first Mississippi. The total distance passed over in the advance was near 1,500 yards.[28]

Although not entirely successful, this precise and well-executed attack was the highlight of the day, if not the whole engagement, to General Granger, who was volubly proud of the courageous behavior of the men of the Fourteenth. They had established an enviable reputation for the regiment. As they marched into the fort, white troops who had watched the maneuver from along the parapet gave them three cheers. It was a memorable moment for the men of the Fourteenth. The first sergeant of Company B turned to Captain Romeyn and said, "Captain, we've got it at last."[28a] The next day the Sixty-eighth Indiana asked to be assigned to Colonel Morgan's command and serve alongside them. As a result, Colonel Doolittle formed a demi-brigade of these two regiments under Morgan's command. Lieutenant Colonel Corbin took command of the Fourteenth U.S. Colored, and Lieutenant Colonel Espy continued in command of the Sixty-eighth.[29]

The infantry attack was devastating to the impotent Confederate artillery batteries. They hadn't seen the attacking force until it was a hundred yards away, and they couldn't turn their guns in that direction. Haskins' two-gun section was the first to be hit. The section commander ordered the men to retreat, and all but two of them ran toward Tarrant's and Darden's batteries on their right. These men joined them in the retreat. Haskins' two guns were spiked, according to Colonel Morgan. One of the two men who couldn't get away from the attack was later found shot and bayoneted in the back; the other was not heard from. Besides the missing man, two were killed and three wounded.

On Haskins' right, Captain Tarrant had to order his men twice before they would abandon their guns. As they moved away, Tarrant approached a group of infantry for help about 150 yards upstream and had a hard time persuading them to fire on the attackers. Captain Darden retreated with his men about 450 yards up the river to a point behind the infantry pickets who had first left the skirmish line and moved back. Of the forty men he had in position at first, his battery lost twenty-one killed and wounded during the day. One of the wounded was Elisha Steele Drake, who was sent home to recover and came back to duty at Selma after the

Nashville Campaign. Two of the battery's ammunition chests were exploded and a caisson ruined.[29a]

The Union attackers were in Haskins' battery position no more than a few minutes. After they retreated, the Confederate picket line was restored and reinforced by the picket reserve. The artillery crews moved back into position with more protection from rifle fire on their left, but cannon fire was still coming at them from three directions. With his right flank taking this much punishment, General Loring requested infantry reinforcements, even though his division was half as large as the entire Federal garrison. The corps commander ordered General French to send Loring a brigade from the Danville Road area. French did as he was ordered and sent Cockrell's Brigade, but he wasn't happy about it. In his diary he noted grumpily that "Loring generally magnifies the enemy's forces."[30]

Meanwhile, there was heavy firing along the entire line that continued all day long, but Hood made no attempt to assault the fort. Union reinforcements continued to arrive and cross the bridge to the fort in full view of Hood's men. The Fourth Michigan under Col. Jairus W. Hall came in from Huntsville, and the 174th Ohio under Col. John S. Jones arrived from Murfreesboro, both by train. The 174th was a brand new regiment organized on 21 September and, Colonel Jones said, had hardly had time to learn the drill formations. The Fourth Michigan had been reorganized on 14 October at Adrian, Michigan, from 726 new men and some veterans, and Decatur was their first duty station. These regiments were just two of the reasons why General Granger told General Thomas that most of his reinforcements were "greener than grass."[31] The Fourth Michigan had no losses at Decatur but later had the same experience as the Third Michigan. In July 1865, they were shipped to Texas where 141 men died of disease on the march from Indianola to San Antonio.[32]

During the action taking place east of the fort, the Confederate troops to the south and southwest had very little to do. Pvt. Thomas J. Stokes of the Tenth Texas of Granbury's Brigade, Cleburne's Division, had time to write a letter to his sister, Mary A.H. Gay of Decatur, Georgia. His regiment was in line of battle about a mile and a quarter southwest of Decatur. He went out reconnoitering in the morning and looked over the enemy's position, which he described as "a large fort immediately in the town with the stars and stripes waving above."[33] Unknown to Stokes, this flag was there partly by courtesy of Pvt. Sampson Ovenden of the Eighteenth Michigan in the fort. At Reveille the flag had become stuck as it was being raised. After a half-dozen unsuccessful tries by several men, including Lieutenant Colonel Thornburgh, to pull it up beyond halfway, Ovenden volunteered because of his previous experience in the navy. He climbed up and unsnagged the lines, but it cost him a serious wound in the thigh from a Confederate sharpshooter. Major Hulburd made special mention in his battle report of Ovenden's bravery.

Stokes wrote that there had been some skirmishing and artillery firing until one hour before, when it seemed to have mostly ceased. He heard distant artillery firing that he supposed was Forrest at Huntsville. They had half rations on Thursday and none by 3:00 p.m. on Friday at the time he wrote but expected some that night, he said. Stokes was chaplain of the regiment as well as rifleman. He was killed later at Franklin, thirty yards from the Federal works.[34]

In the same brigade, Capt. Samuel T. Foster of the Twenty-fourth Texas saw nothing to write about in his diary this day except the food situation. Disgustedly, he said they had nothing to eat since Thursday morning, and "today a wagon drives through the camp and issues two ears of corn to each man."[35] He was from Oakville, Texas. The Fifth Tennessee of Strahl's Brigade, Brown's Division in Cheatham's Corps, was even less fortunate. By the time they got their issue of corn it was only one ear per man. They resorted to parching and eating or making "coffee" from the acorns they could find under the oak trees. They also picked up grains of corn dropped by the artillery horses and roasted them in the ashes of the camp fires. Lt. E.H. Reynolds of Company K said their mounted officers had to guard their horses to prevent corn from being stolen from them. On the twenty-fourth and twenty-fifth this regiment had been in the lead of the army, a position which enabled them to buy apples, potatoes, sorghum and other luxuries along the roadside. Now their gnawing hunger raised protests and muttered threats of refusal if they were ordered to attack the fort.

One group of Confederate soldiers chopped down a large persimmon tree behind the home of a family named Kelly and ate the fruit. The twelve-year-old Kelly boy watched and followed along with them as they continued to their camp. They invited him to eat a supper of corn with them. Sumner A. Cunningham, an officer in Company B of the Forty-first Tennessee in this brigade, still recalled their hunger with

strong feelings for years afterward. It was "the greatest priva-
tion for food we ever had in Dixie," he said.[36] His regiment
only received one ear of corn to four men. Besides acorns they
tried to take the edge off their hunger with some crab apples
and huckleberries they found. After the war Cunningham
became the first editor and manager of "The Confederate
Veteran" magazine.[37]

That morning from Hobson's Island, four miles above
Whitesburg, Master Gilbert Morton on the gunboat *General
Thomas* reported to Colonel Lyon at Huntsville that the river
was rising and had risen one inch in the past twenty-four
hours. If he could force the vessel over the bar he would be at
Decatur in the afternoon. Lyon relayed this message to General Granger and added that the boat had already reached
Whitesburg and left there for Decatur. At 3:00 p.m. the
General Thomas arrived and joined the *Stone River* upstream of
the Confederate artillery. General Granger sent word to the
boats to engage the enemy's river batteries in cooperation with
Captain Beach's guns on the north bank and the gun in the
earthwork east of the fort. From relative safety upstream the
gunboats could fire on the shore batteries while Captain
Beach's two guns fired on them from the opposite shore. The
gun in the Union earthwork was firing from the west, making
a three-way crossfire. Beach reported that his shots dismantled
two of the Confederate guns and caused many casualties.[38]

By 4:30 p.m. the men in the shore batteries had returned
to their guns still under heavy fire from sharpshooters and the
two guns. Cowan's Battery was ready and undamaged above
them on the river, and Kolb's Alabama Battery had reached a
position three miles above Decatur. At this time the gunboats

started downriver. Kolb opened fire on them just as they moved away. He fired twelve rounds of solid shot and soon after was ordered back to camp. When the *General Thomas* came abreast of Cowan's Battery, he opened fire on both boats and got off thirty-two shots, striking them several times without casualties of his own.[39]

As they dropped downstream, the boats fired broadside at the Confederate emplacements. After firing a broadside a gunboat would turn its bow toward the shore and fire its two Parrott rifled guns, then turn back downstream and repeat the cycle. At times during these maneuvers the boats would put on full power, churning the water into a froth behind them. Low shots from the Confederate batteries would hit the water and ricochet toward them. The *Stone River* exploded an enemy caisson and reported killing seventeen men.[40]

Further downstream, Darden's Battery fired on the boats but did little or no damage. Tarrant's Battery fired three shots and got two hits, and Hoskins was able to fire five shots at them, two striking the boats. One crewman aboard the *General Thomas* was mortally wounded in the head, and two others were seriously wounded. On the *Stone River* one man was killed and nine wounded.[41]

During the artillery exchange Darden's Battery fired salvos at the enemy gun on the opposite shore, forcing the enemy infantry to take cover in the earthwork. Lt. Frank Gillette of the Fourteenth U.S. Colored was mortally wounded by a piece of shell.[42]

General Granger watched the gunboat barrage from the shore not far from his headquarters. Some of the guns on the boats were overshooting their targets and the shells were bursting in the air. Granger had a high voice, and in the excitement he ran down to the riverbank shouting, "Lower your pieces," at the boats a mile away, to the amusement of some nearby soldiers.[43]

As he described the action in his battle report, General Granger said that the concentrated Union crossfire made it impossible for the Confederates in the shore batteries to withstand this attack. Some of them retreated to their main infantry line, and some ran down the riverbank to the protection of the trees at the water's edge. The gunboats fired double shots of canister at these men from a distance of 300 yards. Many were killed and some of their bodies later found in the river. This artillery battle of the gunboats only lasted thirty minutes, but it caused severe casualties among Hood's units, according to General Granger's report. In a letter to General Steedman the next day he gave the figure "full 500" in killed and wounded.[44]

Rifle fire from both sides continued all around the fort during the rest of the day. Pvt. George Brooner of the Tenth Indiana Cavalry was killed. Cannons in the fort fired at the Confederate lines any time a group of men was seen large enough to make a target. About 5:00 p.m. 100 men of the Seventy-third Indiana and detachments of other units were sent out under cover of the gathering darkness to dig a new line of rifle pits closer to enemy lines on the east side. After dark the two guns on the north bank of the river were recalled to the fort, but Major Vail remained there with his two infantry companies. On the assumption that the Confederate shore batteries would complete their works during the night, these men moved upstream a short distance and worked all night on a new earthwork with embrasures for three heavy guns. Just before dawn they were ordered back to the fort.[45]

On the Confederate side, Pvt. Cary H. Wilkinson, a Mississippian who had been wounded on the twenty-sixth, was wounded again by a shell on the twenty-eighth. He probably was another casualty of the gunboats' artillery. Pvt. Reuben Nations (FIG. 14) of the Twelfth Louisiana in Scott's Brigade was scouting Union positions in front of Loring's Division when he was hit by a shell from the fort. It shattered his legs below the knee, and both legs had to be amputated. He was from Whitfield County, Georgia.[46]

Lt. W.H. Berryhill of the Forty-third Mississippi had seen the afternoon artillery battle with the gunboats but was not much impressed. Later he wrote to his wife, "There was nothing done but sharp-shooting and shelling each other and running batteries up at different points on the river to shell the gunboats. They moved their position every time our guns were brought to bear on them." He thought they could have taken the fort, but it would have cost more lives than it was worth. General Hood had issued an order to the troops when they started on the campaign that he wouldn't force them to charge any strongly fortified positions, he said, "but the troops would have pitched into this place very willingly from all that I could see or hear."[47] His regiment had twelve men killed and three wounded in the Decatur fight. Berryhill was later killed at Nashville, shot through the head. He was thirty-six years old and the father of seven children, the youngest of whom he had never seen.[48]

In Huntsville, Mrs. Chadick noted that many wounded Union soldiers were brought in from Decatur on Thursday night, and eighty Confederate prisoners were brought in that Friday evening.[49]

Late that night a dense fog formed over the area giving Hood's men an ideal cover as they began their withdrawal, but it couldn't hide the noisy business in the artillery batteries as guns, caissons and horses were hitched up. To mask this activity a section of the Confederate line on the east spent the greater part of the night digging a line of rifle pits closer to the fort. Lieutenant Colonel Corbin and 250 men of the Fourteenth U.S. Colored occupied a line of picket posts in front of the Confederates to observe them, but the artillery got away without their knowing it.[50]

After the afternoon artillery battle, the *General Thomas* landed at Decatur. From the landing she fired six shots before 6:00 p.m., then cast loose after dark and anchored in the river. From 8:00 p.m. to midnight her log read: "Weather clear; wind S.W." and from 12:00 to 4:00 a.m.: "Weather cold with heavy fog," then at 3:00 a.m. the entry: "The enemy removed their batteries from the bank of the river. Continued firing of the pickets."[51]

From his position near Gadsden, General Wheeler again reported the movement of Sherman's Fourth Corps to Chattanooga and the position of his main army, which that morning was still at Gaylesville. Union prisoners captured by Wheeler's men believed Sherman would march to Savannah or Mobile, he said. At this time Wheeler was sending three to five dispatches each day, both by courier line directly to Hood and by courier and telegraph via Blue Mountain, Selma,

Corinth and Tuscumbia, trying to keep Hood informed of Sherman's dispositions.[52]

At General Garth's home that morning both Hood and Beauregard had reached the point of frustration by the lack of information about Forrest's cavalry. Since leaving Gadsden, General Beauregard had received a delayed message from Forrest dated 21 October at Jackson, Tennessee, stating he was about to cross the river and push for Nashville. Yet seven days later there had been no word from him and no sign that he had done this. Adding to the dilemma, Forrest's message had said the enemy division at Clifton had departed and was hastening with all speed back to Huntsville. Hood was at a decision point which depended heavily on Forrest, and Beauregard must have finally decided that the Tennessee Campaign couldn't wait for the completion of what he supposed was Forrest's mission against the railroad. Early that morning he dispatched an amended order directly to Forrest, bypassing General Taylor (whom he notified the next day), this time "desiring" Forrest to report to Hood at once instead of after completing his mission. But again his order lacked immediacy and was subject to misinterpretation. Hoping to contact Forrest on another tack, Hood directed General Roddey to get word to him to meet the army at Bainbridge Crossing. By this time Forrest was still on the west bank of the river approaching Fort Heiman, thirty miles north of Jackson, Tennessee near the Kentucky line.[53]

Army engineers reported to General Hood that there was no other crossing point nearer than Courtland, twenty miles to the west, and it would be a difficult one. The problem, according to one source, was a shortage of pontoons for bridging the river. Based on this news he met with General Beauregard, and they discussed the army's next move. Apparently they had a difference of opinion about it, but in the end Hood decided to abandon the Decatur crossing and move downriver to cross at Bainbridge, ten miles from Tuscumbia. At this point he still intended to return to Stevenson after crossing the river. A Union prisoner who was working in Hood's headquarters on the twenty-eighth overheard this conversation. He escaped on the thirtieth and reported to General Granger that Hood had wanted to continue the siege and assault the fort, but Beauregard decided this would not be practicable.[54]

Beauregard and his staff left for Courtland late in the morning and established headquarters there by the end of the day. Before leaving he advised Richmond, by a message that didn't reach there until 31 October, that the army would leave that evening and the next day for Bainbridge to cross the river and that nothing positive was known of the position of Sherman's army. During a busy afternoon Hood took time to plan his disengagement and the next day's movement.[55]

Up to this time General Sherman hadn't taken action to move the two divisions of Maj. Gen. A.J. Smith's corps in Missouri to General Thomas' command. That morning, 28 October, he asked General Halleck in Washington for reinforcements for Thomas, and Halleck's order reached Major General Rosecrans the same day to direct the movement of Smith's corps. These men would have to march across the whole state of Missouri to St. Louis, then take boat transportation to reach Nashville. Sherman didn't think they could reach Thomas in less than ten days (they got to St. Louis on

24 November), yet he still held on to all of his remaining corps for his own campaign. Overnight he had come to the conclusion that Hood wasn't going to cross the river at Decatur, and early on the twenty-eighth he ordered the four corps present with him to move east to Rome, Georgia, beginning in the afternoon so as to reach there the next day.[56]

Sherman and his staff left Gaylesville on the same morning and reached Rome late in the day. From there he fired off a burst of messages to Generals Thomas and Granger with new instructions and estimates of the situation. He ordered Granger to hold on to the death. Hood was low on ammunition and couldn't afford to attack fortified places, he said. He believed Hood was at Decatur for the purpose of repairing the railroad from Corinth to Tuscumbia, was short of supplies and couldn't waste men on an assault. Also, he thought Hood had changed his supply base from Jacksonville to Tuscumbia and would probably cross the river at Lamb's Ferry or Bainbridge. Thus, while Hood and Beauregard were still uncertain where the Union army was, Sherman had zeroed in on Hood's problems and intentions with near-perfect accuracy. He was now communicating freely by telegraph north of the river all along Hood's route, while Hood had to depend for intelligence on the fifty mile courier route from General Wheeler.[57]

CHAPTER SEVEN

Counting Railroad Ties
Toward Tuscumbia

A T 1:00 A.M. ON SATURDAY THE TWENTY-NINTH, SGT. John Maddock and a detachment of forty-two men of Battery D, First Missouri Light Artillery, arrived from Huntsville to reinforce the fort. They brought two brass howitzers, a twelve pounder and a twenty-four pounder. The twelve pounder was put in Fort No. 2, and the twenty-four pounder in Fort No. 1 on the west face of the works. After sunup Sergeant Maddock directed the twenty-four pounder at groups of Hood's men in the ravine at 800 yards, and on the crest of the hill and the woods 1,800 yards to the south. Maddock and his men brought the strength of the garrison to 5,000 men.[1]

Toward morning Colonel Morgan of the Fourteenth U.S. Colored reported to Colonel Doolittle that he was hearing sounds of unusual movements that made him suspect the Confederates were making a move toward the west. Hoping this might be a sign the enemy was withdrawing, Doolittle ordered him to make a reconnaissance to find out what they were doing. Morgan led his regiment out of the fort as soon as it was light. They covered the ground in front of the east and center of the fort until they came up to an enemy rear guard force. The Confederates opened a brisk infantry fire against their skirmishers, and almost immediately Lt. Charles

Woodworth, who was standing beside Colonel Morgan, was shot through the face and fell dead. Morgan formed a battle line just behind the crest of a ridge and sent skirmishers forward while an officer went back to headquarters for instructions. General Granger sent Lieutenant Colonel Atkinson with 400 men of the Third Michigan out to the picket line behind the position of the Fourteenth to cover their retreat and ordered Colonel Morgan to withdraw. By 7:30 a.m. Morgan had reported his observations to headquarters.[2]

While Colonel Morgan's reconnaissance force was still out, General Granger rode around the lines and found his troops in splendid spirits. He wired General Thomas that fog enveloped the enemy but their line of skirmishers was still visible 800 yards away. He had heard Confederate bugles at daylight and he could still hear an occasional cheer from them, he said. They presented a line two and a half to three miles long, thoroughly entrenched, and had been felt very heavily on the east and west. It wasn't until 10:00 a.m., when lookouts spotted a Confederate column two miles to the south and moving west, that he decided he could report to General Thomas that Hood was withdrawing. Later, from the roof of his headquarters he could see a thin line of departing Rebels three miles long. He learned from his pickets downstream that Hood's wagon trains and artillery had moved out and around to the west between 1:00 and 4:00 a.m. on the Courtland Road.[3]

The Confederate brigades pulled back regiment by regiment all day long, beginning on the east of the line, and circled to the south and around to the railroad tracks on the west. The Twelfth Louisiana of Scott's Brigade was one of the earliest to pull out. At daylight Capt. Evander M. Graham received orders to withdraw. As soon as their pickets were relieved by the Fifty-fifth Alabama, they fell back slowly to the rear. After moving back some distance, they marched to the south and then west and joined the command marching down the railroad. Corporal Bevens of the First Arkansas remembered that they nearly froze to death the night before, but now they were grateful for the frozen ground. It was easier for marching than mud. They took up the march on the Memphis and Charleston railroad and moved parallel to the dirt road to Courtland, "counting railroad ties" as they called it. General Hood had left at daylight and was in Courtland by 1:00 p.m. Stewart's Corps marched toward a campsite three miles from Courtland on a farm owned by Mr. Swoope (but occupied by Mr. Watkins), and Cheatham's men followed toward the same position.[4]

Leaving a small rear guard on the skirmish line, Stewart's Corps was on the march while it was still morning, French's Division behind Loring's and Walthal's divisions. General French was struck by the destruction and desolation that he and his staff saw on every side as they rode beside the railroad. He wrote in his journal that night, "The country is beautiful and the soil is rich; but what a desolation everywhere! The dreamy silence, the absence of life, the smoky atmosphere, the abandoned dwellings, the uncultivated fields, the destruction of fences — everything, everywhere mark the ravages of war that has changed this once beautiful valley of the Tennessee into a desert in all save the rich soil .... The only signs of life are here and there a rabbit startled from ambush, and now and then a solitary crow perched on a dead limb of a tree."[4]

Following Stewart, Cheatham's Corps stopped at dark nine miles from Decatur and made camp. The next morning as they approached Courtland, an animated lady on horseback rode up to the Forty-first Tennessee and greeted the men with smiles and cheerful waves. She was Miss Maggie Whiteside from Shelbyville. Many of the men tipped their hats and bowed to her as they passed. Sumner A. Cunningham of Company B had high praise for what he said were her incessant efforts for the morale of the men of the "lost cause," and she would be remembered by many thousands of soldiers and officers.[4b]

On the afternoon of the twenty-ninth, Ross's Brigade of Jackson's Cavalry Division rode up to the southwest of the fort at Decatur and dismounted to form a line facing the fort. Of each four men, three joined the skirmish line and the fourth led the horses to the rear and held them in a safe position. They had left Cave Springs, Georgia, on 24 October via Gadsden on the twenty-fifth on an exhausting ride to join the Army, and were stopped at Decatur to guard the rear of the departing troops.

A short time later, Lumsden's, Tarrant's and Selden's Alabama batteries of Trueheart's Battalion passed to the south of them within sight of Decatur. Tarrant's battery was ordered to move up under cover of the cavalry line and fire at the fort to hold the Federals in place. Their shots were returned by the deadly accurate fire of the three-inch rifled guns in the fort, making their open positions extremely hazardous. Sgt. James R. Maxwell of Tuscaloosa, Alabama, a gunner in Lumsden's Battery, said these guns were as accurate as any long range hand rifle. Late in the day when the *General Thomas* joined in with a few shots against the Confederate battery, this became a small artillery duel.[5]

After the area east of the fort had cleared of Confederates, Lieutenant McTeer of the Third Tennessee Cavalry scouted over the places where the fighting had been heaviest the day before. He was shocked by the signs of great destruction of life where the infantry assault and the artillery battle had occurred. The trench across the mound behind the Confederate shore batteries was drenched with blood. In the places where artillery ammunition cases had been blown up, pieces of bone and flesh from the size of a hand down to small pieces were scattered over the ground. Some uncompleted graves three or four feet long were piled with parts of the bodies of men blown to pieces by explosions. They were marked by boards listing the names and commands of the men. A hat lay burned to a crisp and filled with the remains of a soldier's head. The body of a Confederate artillery man lay near the river about fifteen feet from the remains of a caisson. It was so badly burned that brass buttons could be plucked easily from the uniform.[6]

By 4:00 p.m. only a thin rear guard was left on the Confederate skirmish line, and by dark the Federal troops reoccupied their original outer lines. Except for minor rear guard actions, the siege of Decatur was over. When the west side of the fort was clear, some skirmishers of the Seventy-third Indiana recovered the body of Pvt. Robert Flewellen who was killed on the twenty-seventh. They found several Confederates' bodies left unburied in their gopher holes. Colonel Doolittle took advantage of the lull in the action by moving back into his headquarters, which he had vacated previously when a shell passed directly through his dining room. At dark a combined force of 950 men was sent out on the Courtland Road under Col. J.W. Hall of the Fourth Michigan. Two miles out they met a strong picket line of Confederates that halted them, and they returned to the fort late at night.[7]

On the previous day General Lee had marched his corps to a campsite three miles from Courtland. On the twenty-ninth, Hood sent him orders to move on to Leighton, ten miles further west. Shortly afterwards he received another order from Hood to move to Bainbridge Crossing early the next day to assist the engineers in laying a bridge. Without stopping at Leighton, Lee marched on to Bainbridge, and during the night sent three brigades across the river in pontoon boats near Florence. The next afternoon they drove off Brigadier General Croxton's brigade of 1000 cavalry that was occupying the town.[8]

From reports of this activity which he received on the night of the twenty-ninth, General Granger telegraphed General Thomas at 9:45 p.m. that he didn't think this could be Hood's advance, since they wouldn't have had time to get to Florence. Up to this point his predictions of Hood's intentions and movements had been almost uniformly wrong. Smarting over this unfortunate record, he made a final effort to vindicate himself in his after-action report on 6 November but only made matters worse. Concerning his message to General Thomas on 26 October he wrote "I did not think the attack upon Decatur as yet serious, as it could hardly be more than the advance of Hood's army the entire of it not having had time to arrive before Decatur. My suppositions proved correct, as the attack was made by a detachment of Walthal's Division of Stewart's Corps."[9]

General Granger reported 113 Federal casualties during the action at Decatur. Based on information from prisoners, citizens and other sources, he estimated Confederate losses to be at least 1,000. A captured Union soldier working at Confederate headquarters said positively that he heard General Hood admit to 1,000 casualties in killed and wounded alone, and a war correspondent there reported 1,500 losses to a Mobile newspaper.[10]

In Confederate records for this time, only General Stewart's periodic report gives a first-hand casualty figure indicative of the army's losses at Decatur. In a brief mention of the fight he wrote, "We next encountered the enemy at Decatur, Ala. toward the end of October, driving in his pickets and skirmishing a day or two, with a loss of some 135 men, but making no serious attack on his strongly entrenched position."[11] Stewart's only division commander to report on the engagement, Major General Walthal, was almost non-committal: "Some skirmishing and considerable artillery firing occurred every day while we were there, but without results, except the loss of a few men."[12] Allowing for errors and exaggerations, Hood's casualties in killed, wounded and captured were probably several hundred, possibly more than 1,000.[13]

All that was left to mark the Army of Tennessee's action at Decatur were hundreds of rifle pits circling the fort and a wide ring of trampled earth a mile or so from town where 23,000 men had bivouacked. Ashes from old camp fires and the poor refuse left from the camps of the ragged soldiers dotted the area. Here and there along this line were the shallow graves of the men who were killed, identified by wooden crosses or upended boards. Later some family member might come in a wagon to search the area and take his soldier's remains home, but this must have been difficult. During much of 1864 every road leading from Decatur was vigilantly picketed to prevent both Union and Confederate deserters from reaching the mountains south of Decatur where they congregated around Day's Gap, a short distance southeast of Danville.[14]

Some of the dead probably remained until after the war and a few perhaps forever. Some grave markers were knocked down by livestock, and it was said that slaves sometimes removed them as a silent protest. Confederate dead around the shore batteries and other areas exposed to fire were left on the field to be buried by Union men from the fort. The Confederate government sent no formal notices to the relatives of the deceased. They were usually informed by the soldier's comrades, a company commander, chaplain or relative in the army, or through casualty lists published in newspapers.[15]

Joel D. Murphree (FIG. 11) of Troy, Alabama, Quartermaster Sergeant of the Fifty-seventh Alabama of Scott's Brigade, Loring's Division, wrote his wife in Tuscumbia that most of the wounded were left in the hands of the enemy for lack of transportation. One of these was Joseph E. Mills of Troy who had a flesh wound in the thigh. T.R. Trotter, Assistant Surgeon of the Fifteenth Mississippi of Adams' Brigade, Loring's Division, was one of those left behind to care for the Confederate wounded. He became a prisoner of the Federal garrison.[16]

General Sherman, still in Rome, telegraphed orders to General Thomas that day that if the enemy crossed the

Tennessee in force, he should abandon all minor points and concentrate his forces at some point where he could cover the road from Murfreesboro to Stevenson. Thomas could abandon Huntsville and that line, if necessary, but he wanted Decatur and Chattanooga held. In a dispatch to Washington he told General Halleck that he had sent the 4th Corps to reinforce Thomas and might send Schofield's 23rd Corps as well, but he didn't want to go back himself with the whole army, since that was what the enemy wanted.[17]

CHAPTER EIGHT

A Reckoning

THE FEDERAL COMMAND WAS JUSTLY PROUD OF ITS conduct at the siege of Decatur in holding out against Hood's army. General Granger and Colonel Doolittle directed the defense skillfully and with an aggressiveness that surprised Hood's men. A Confederate artillery officer later told Colonel Doolittle they at first thought the fort had only a small defensive force, but when they were met so boldly with cavalry, they believed it had been reinforced. General Granger reported that captured officers said they never saw cavalry stand up so bravely before infantry. They would not be stampeded.[1]

The inexperienced men in the fort fought bravely in defying an enemy force never less than four times the size of their own. Only Capt. James C. Wilson of the Thirteenth Indiana merited censure for reasons not specified in battle reports. He was placed in arrest and charges were preferred against him. (He was dropped from the rolls on 31 December for other infractions.) Several officers were promoted for their parts in the battle. The list included both Granger and Doolittle, Col. William Given of the 102nd Ohio, and Lt. Col. Henry C. Corbin of the Fourteenth U.S. Colored. In his battle report Colonel Doolittle recommended that the units which fought there be authorized to inscribe "Decatur" on their regimental flags. The Seventy-third Indiana, for one, did this.[2]

Hood's men did everything that was asked of them and fought with spirit and determination under the orders they were given. The men on the east and west of the fort saw desperate action at times, some of the regiments and batteries taking casualties on a scale that might be expected in a major battle. Even the units on the southern sector of the line took a share of casualties from cannon and rifle fire. According to General Granger, Confederate prisoners told them that wherever the fort's shells and sharpshooters could reach, they suffered heavy loss.[3]

But most of Hood's men remembered this engagment as a time of hunger and miserable discomfort, a time of lying in cold, muddy rifle pits on the picket line or in vedette posts, dodging bullets and watching the enemy across the sodden fields. Except for some mutinous grumbling about the shortage of food, they endured these hardships manfully, waiting for orders to assault the fort but not comprehending why it might be necessary. A.L. Orr of the Eighteenth Texas Cavalry (dismounted), Cleburne's Division, wrote to his sister in Ellis County, Texas, expressing the typically uncritical sentiment of the soldiers about the engagement: "We serounded the place and staid there three days, though did not try to take it. We could of taken it but would of lost a grate many men."[4] In his final report on the campaign General Beauregard paid high tribute to these men. "Untoward and calamitous as were the issues of the campaign, never in the course of this war have the best qualities of our soldiery been more conspicuously shown; never more enthusiasm evinced than when the troops once more crossed the Tennessee River," he wrote.[5]

The direction of the battlefield action by General Hood and some of his commanders was less praiseworthy. General Stewart on the right flank was surprised by the enemy twice in one day, once by the Union artillery attack from the north bank of the river and again by the infantry attack on his shore batteries. General Loring and General Featherston failed to support the batteries and thus nullified their efforts to break the pontoon bridge. There was a near-total lack of coordination between them and the artillery, according to the battery commanders. Captain Darden reported that he didn't see a general or field grade officer all day long after Lieutenant Colonel Williams left him at daylight. In his report, Captain Tarrant stated that "some officer was highly culpable for the disgraceful affairs of the day" and recommended that an investigation be made.[5a] Lieutenant Colonel Williams expressed a similar but less blunt opinion in his report to General Stewart. Stewart himself was slow and ineffective in responding to the situation developing on his right flank. No one seemed to have considered the risk of artillery attack from the north bank, despite the activity there that must have been detectable on the twenty-seventh.[5b]

General Cleburne's reputation as the best division commander in the Confederacy lost some of its luster on the twenty-eighth when Captain Moore's small force routed the Confederate picket line on the west of the fort. His failure to guard the concealed approach along the riverbank cost many casualties and must have disrupted whatever purpose General Hood had intended by tightening the siege of the fort. The

Confederate commanders were not expecting the fort to take such aggressive action and had allowed themselves to become careless in the face of the small enemy force. (It has been said that Cleburne probably would have been promoted to command III Corps instead of Stewart had it not been for his support of a politically unpopular idea for filling the army's depleted ranks. He and some other officers recommended that freed slaves who volunteered be taken into the army.)[6]

Hood's tactical generalship was clouded by uncharacteristic indecisiveness and by several unaccountable decisions which seem contrary to his purposes. The usual explanation for his failure to take the fort on the first or second day is that it was too strongly defended, but this is unconvincing. When Stewart's Corps arrived, the fort's outer defenses were unmanned and it was clearly not at the ready. In a situation obviously calling for artillery, Hood only used twelve guns while spending the afternoon fully deploying an infantry corps of 11,600 men. Colonel Doolittle and Captain Beach estimated the attacking artillery as one battery of four or five guns, perhaps an indication of their moderate rate of fire. Doolittle reported that he fought on the twenty-sixth with less than 500 men, two of his regiments not being engaged. At first only two of his guns were in action. Stewart's Corps alone could have mounted thirty-six guns against the fort. Doolittle thought it was miraculous that they could escape capture. "If we had been subject to a heavy fire of artillery it would have been almost impossible to remain," he said.[7] Some of the other officers thought the fort could have been taken easily on the first day.[8]

The pontoon bridge was an important target that could have been broken the first or second day without great risk to

Confederate guns if covered by fire from the other artillery, even without an earthwork. The delay in attacking the bridge until the twenty-eighth resulted in the artillery's inability to even fire at it. The Union garrison would have been strongly inclined to surrender if they had been isolated from reinforcements, but General Granger never knew the bridge had been targeted. In a letter to General James B. Steedman on the thirtieth he wrote, "It is a remarkable fact that with eight pieces of artillery within easy range of the bridge and our men crossing it continually, they never once fired on it."9

This hesitant approach to Decatur was out of character for one of the Confederacy's strongest adherents of offensive tactics. General Hood confirmed later that he did not "attack" Decatur, but it was almost certainly not the aggressive defense put up by the fort's small garrison that held him to a costly and unproductive demonstration. In the days spent marching across Alabama he must have become more and more aware that his change in route was developing serious complications. Since leaving Gadsden, he expected every day to hear that Forrest's cavalry was en route toward his vicinity. By the time the army reached Decatur and he still had no word from Forrest, he may have already decided to postpone commitment by investing the fort and waiting for him.10

At this stage Hood's plan hinged on reaching Stevenson ahead of any large force Sherman might send to give battle or to reinforce General Thomas. Speed of movement was imperative and was growing more critical each day. A river crossing at Guntersville would have put the army close enough to Stevenson to capture the railroad junction there with infantry while Sherman was south of the river. From Decatur this had become a far more difficult and risky choice. If Sherman decided to move to Stevenson through Bridgeport, he now had more time and was closer to it than the Confederates. Suddenly Hood's need for cavalry had become more urgent. More than for guarding the wagon train, he needed cavalry to do what he had postponed doing earlier: break the bridge at Bridgeport and the railroad east of Stevenson. Evidently he didn't believe Jackson's small cavalry division was up to this task or perhaps was essential to guard his advance after crossing the river.

Although Forrest wasn't expected to be at Decatur in the few days since the Gadsden meeting, the absence of any word from him created a dilemma that paralyzed Hood. By this time, if he ordered Wheeler at Gadsden to attack the bridge, he would be exposing his right and would widen Wheeler's separation from the army. Wheeler would be at risk of being cut off by Sherman's forces at Gaylesville. In a message to President Davis on 12 November Hood merely said he needed Wheeler to look after his right flank. General Forrest had already been requested to attack the railroad north of Stevenson and, for all Hood knew, might be en route to do this. All he could do about this problem was to wait on word from Forrest. But it didn't come.[11]

It was the second of November before General Beauregard finally sent Forrest a long-overdue peremptory order from Tuscumbia "directing" him to come at once — what he should have done at the beginning.[12] Hood followed this with his own plaintive message, "When can I expect you here or when can I hear from you? I am waiting for you."[13] These messages at last produced an unenthusiastic response from

Forrest in his report to General Taylor on 3 November. He would comply with the order unless it was countermanded, he said, as soon as the worn condition of his horses would permit and he could gather his scattered command. He thought his blockade of the river would be more advantageous to the campaign than anything. His wagons and artillery were mired in deep mud, and he didn't arrive in Tuscumbia until the fourteenth.[14]

Undoubtedly it was the great success of his raid at Johnsonville that gave Forrest reason for wanting to continue his operations on the west bank. He had destroyed four gunboats, fourteen transports, twenty barges, twenty-six artillery pieces, and had burned nearly a mile of warehouses along the wharf with 75,000-120,000 tons of stores. He had captured 150 prisoners, 9,000 pairs of shoes and 1,000 blankets. The Union garrison of 1,000 men had panicked and fled toward Nashville. His own casualties were two killed and nine wounded, the enemy's an estimated 500.[15]

Not long after turning toward Decatur, Hood began to recognize that he had another problem that was rapidly growing even more serious than his need for cavalry. As the soldiers' complaints of hunger reminded him, the army's logistics condition was reaching a precarious state. By adding ten to fifteen days to the march to Stevenson, the detour to Decatur had radically changed the circumstances of his supply plan. The twenty days of supplies in the wagon train would have supported a quick movement through Guntersville to Stevenson and into Tennessee where food was available. At Decatur, with a good part of the rations already consumed, he would be lucky to muster enough to return to Stevenson.

Unless he gambled on this thin margin, he would need the base at Tuscumbia immediately as a primary source of supply, not merely as the backup source he had planned in case of defeat in Tennessee. But Tuscumbia had no stores of food or ammunition and, as Beauregard had feared, nothing had arrived there since the base was changed from Jacksonville. It must have been the twenty-eighth when they found out the warehouses were still empty. Beginning then and for many days afterwards, both Hood and Beauregard flooded the courier line and telegraph wires with their messages trying to get rations sent to Tuscumbia.[16]

All of these efforts and those of General Taylor had no results other than to reveal the miserable conditions of the rail-roads. All supplies for the Army would have to come from the south on the creaky Mobile and Ohio Railroad to Corinth, Mississippi, then to Tuscumbia on the Memphis and Charleston. It seemed to be a surprise to Hood when he learned that the last fifteen-mile stretch of this track from Cherokee, Alabama, to Tuscumbia was still completely unusable. It was not put in running order until 21 November. His own wagons would have to carry the load from Cherokee on a dirt road that was nearly impassable in rainy weather. His earlier request to General Bragg to have the railroad repaired from Tuscumbia to Decatur had not been implemented, and the path as far as Courtland where those tracks had been was nothing but a long strip of weeds. From Courtland to Decatur the railroad was not badly damaged.[17]

Up to now the army had been moving with an "expedi-tion" type of wagon supply where wagons started a mission with supplies for a specified period and stayed with the troops until returning to base or reaching a new source of supply. If he decided now to rely on Tuscumbia for food supplies as well as ammunition, Hood would have to establish immediately a full-scale, circulating "supply train" system all the way from Cherokee to Tuscumbia, then through Decatur to the rear of the Army. Even if he established a forward supply base at Decatur, a train of this length would take a great many more horses and wagons.[18]

The train had been several hundred wagons short of requirements from the start at Palmetto. It had been on the move for a month at top speed with the drivers under orders not to water animals while on the march. As a result, the horses and mules frequently were not watered at all and sometimes not fed by the weary teamsters. One group of wagons traveled seven days without unharnessing and didn't average one feeding per day, according to Major E.W. Ewing, the army's transportation inspector. By the time they reached Tuscumbia, Ewing estimated that 1,500 replacements were needed for worn-down animals, yet Hood wouldn't allow officers' horses to be taken for this purpose. Many of the horses captured from the enemy from time to time were being sold off or traded by the men who captured them. "Everything is in greater confusion than I have ever seen it," Ewing concluded.[19]

On top of this, at Decatur General Hood's ammunition supply problem still had not gone away. In fact, the lack of a reserve supply within reach must have been one reason for his restrained use of artillery to reduce the enemy garrison, just as General Sherman suspected. When he learned that no supplies had reached the Tuscumbia base, it certainly must have crossed his mind that a bombardment of the fort would use quantities of ammunition that couldn't be replaced. Artillery would be needed very shortly to attack the several blockhouses on the railroad to Stevenson and the Stevenson defenses. In any case, ordnance supply remained a potentially critical problem until 29 October when ten carloads of ammunition were shipped from Selma toward Tuscumbia, too late to affect the planned crossing at Decatur. Ordnance supply problems were to plague the army during the rest of the campaign and became desperate for a time at Nashville.[20]

As Sherman described Hood's situation in a message to General Thomas on the 29th, "I don't see how Beauregard can support his army; but Jeff Davis is desperate, and, his men will undertake anything possible,"[21] and to General Halleck on 3 November he wrote, "The country round about Florence has been again and again devastated during the past three years, and Beauregard must be dependent on the Mobile and Ohio Railroad, which has been broken and patched up in its whole extent."[22]

Without the slightest doubt the army was all but logistics-bound. It was nearing the condition described by the fourth century writer Vegetius: "Time and Opportunity may help to retrieve other Misfortunes; but where Forage and Provisions have not been carefully provided, the Evil is without Remedy."[23] Strategy had become a distant second priority to supply and transportation considerations. Hood either had to abandon his planned route or move ahead and gamble on reaching Tennessee, where he believed he could live off the land, quickly. (He did live off the land there to a considerable extent in November and December.)[24]

When the out-of-position wagons could catch up at
Decatur, the army still had rations for perhaps ten days. If
General Hood crossed the river now, this would have to last
for the six or seven days of marching back to Stevenson and
beyond. The only other help he could hope for in this vicinity was capturing supplies from the enemy. As it happened,
Decatur could have been the first opportunity for extra food
from this source. General Granger had recently stockpiled a
reserve of 60,000 rations above regular supply levels and a
large amount of ammunition. With his base at Tuscumbia
temporarily nonfunctional, Hood would be taking the same
kind of risk that Sherman was about to take on his march to
the coast — moving without a base and depending on supplying the army from the country — but from a far more
austere starting condition and through an area long since
stripped of supplies.[25]

From his perspective at Decatur, General Hood may have
been tempted by the direct route to Nashville through Athens
and Pulaski, which beckoned at Decatur Junction just across
the river. It would be shorter by many critical days of march
and closer to the Tuscumbia base and to a junction with
Forrest, but neither he nor Beauregard seemed to give this
the slightest consideration. One obvious argument against
this route was that the bridges and trestles as far as Pulaski
had been destroyed by Forrest a month earlier and would take
sixty days to repair, by Forrest's estimate. More important,
the rail and telegraph connections between Sherman and
Thomas would remain open to threaten the army's right flank
all along the way and eliminate the key part of Hood's
strategy for isolating General Thomas from Sherman. General

Beauregard suggested another reason that must have influenced him to cling to the original route through Stevenson: it was very similar to the plan President Davis had agreed to at Palmetto and had been approved by General Bragg.[26]

While Hood wrestled with these problems at Decatur, undecided whether to gamble on a river crossing, General Thomas had his own problems, just as daunting but of a different kind. With the Army of Tennessee threatening his river line, he had only 7,700 cavalry of General Hatch's Division and Croxton's Brigade and the 12,000 men of the Fourth Corps with which to concentrate a forward defense. Despite Sherman's advice to do so, he couldn't pull out the troops guarding the Memphis and Charleston railroad that General Stanley was about to use to move the 4th Corps. Left unguarded, these tracks would be destroyed in short order by roving cavalry scouts or guerrillas.[27]

The 12,000 raw troops he had received recently as reinforcements, some of which were at Decatur, had not quite offset the 15,000 veterans he had sent home for discharge or to vote. Even as he was anxiously trying to get back the men furloughed to vote, he received a message from Washington on 28 October authorizing him to furlough all men from Illinois to go home and vote. He politely declined. A few days later, he learned that the convalescents from Sherman's army, which he expected would reinforce General Steedman at Chattanooga, had arrived there with approved furloughs in hand and were awaiting transportation home.[28]

Thomas' problems didn't end there. Even with the Fourth Corps on the way to him, his efforts to concentrate were hindered by Forrest's raid in west Tennessee and by Sherman's preemption of the Nashville-Chattanooga railroad. Sherman had the rails tied up in shipping surplus supplies from the Atlanta Campaign to depots in Chattanooga and Nashville.[29]

General Stanley had his Fourth Corps assembled in Chattanooga by 29 October, and he started for Athens the next morning with one division. They got there at 5:00 a.m. on the thirty-first on a train of 150 cars. The supply wagons and artillery, escorted by a brigade of infantry, marched via Decherd and Fayetteville toward Pulaski and arrived a week later. At Athens the men had barely finished unloading from the train when General Stanley received orders at 11:00 a.m. to move on to Pulaski. They began to leave at 2:00 p.m. that afternoon and, after fording the chest-deep waters of Elk River, reached Pulaski the next day. His other two divisions followed and rejoined them on 3 and 4 November.[30]

Just as General Stanley was about to leave Athens, General Granger almost put a crimp in the operation. He advised Stanley by telegraph that his cavalry scouts reported a large Confederate force at Brown's Ferry near Courtland, and he believed they would force a crossing there. At the time he had just received reports that Hood's whole army would return to Decatur the next day and try to take the fort with the help of Wheeler's cavalry, whose advance was already in sight of the pickets east of town. At 3:00 p.m. he ordered the garrison at Athens to destroy their property and supplies and move to Decatur. The men had marched half-way to Decatur by 5:00 p.m., when General Thomas ordered Granger to return them at once. His embarrassed reply was that a train was off the track at Decatur Junction, and he couldn't get transportation. Besides that, the telegraph operator at Athens had left with the troops, General Stanley had taken all the rations with him, and the garrison would have no food. Stanley avoided involvement in the problem and continued with his march. The report of enemy movement proved to be false.[31]

On the thirtieth, General Sherman learned that some of the new regiments promised by General Grant for reinforcing Thomas were coming forward very slowly. That day he ordered Maj. Gen. John M. Schofield and his Twenty-third Corps, 10,000 strong, to follow Stanley to Thomas' command. Schofield was in Rome at the time, after marching from Gaylesville the previous day with the other four corps. As he wrote in his memoirs, "I was three days' march toward Atlanta en route to Savannah when 1 got the order to proceed to the railroad and report to General Thomas."[32]

General Thomas first instructed him to come to Tullahoma, Tennessee, by rail and march to Pulaski, but before he could get there he was ordered to continue to Nashville. When he reached there with one division on 5 November, he was sent immediately to deal with Forrest's raid on the large supply depot at Johnsonville eighty miles due west of Nashville. He left two brigades there and returned to Nashville with one brigade. The rest of his corps was delayed at Dalton by Sherman's supply trains and didn't reach Chattanooga until 7 November and Nashville on the ninth.

The two divisions promised to General Thomas from Missouri were delayed and didn't reach Nashville until 30 November. As one of Sherman's officers later said, "For a week and a half Thomas' forces were scattered over a territory greater than France .... All that seemed lacking to complete the assortment of feeble odds and ends with which Sherman was equipping Thomas was an order to stuff a few thousand uniforms with straw and use them vigorously and judiciously along Hood's front."[33]

In his eagerness to leave General Thomas to take care of Hood and start his own campaign, Sherman was leaving a gap in the Union's defenses better than Hood could have wanted. The road to Stevenson was wide open for a time except for the strung-out Fourth Corps and the small garrisons on the rail-road. Sherman had said he could guard Bridgeport better from Rome than any other point, but the railroad bridge there was a fragile target, easier to attack than defend. If he couldn't concentrate enough force to stop Hood at Stevenson, he took the chance of having to chase the Confederate Army from behind while it "retreated" to Nashville. When Sherman decided against this and retired to Kingston, Brig. Gen. Jacob D. Cox, a division commander in the Twenty-third Corps, thought it "an act of moral courage to risk the terrible and far-reaching consequences of this move."[34] But another Union officer regarded it as abandoning the objective Grant had given him to destroy Hood's army. "Leaving this job to Thomas was equivalent to abandoning the country from Nashville to Atlanta which had taken two years to secure as far as Chattanooga," he wrote.[35]

The disorganized condition of the Union defenses along the river may well have been academic to General Hood because of his own crushing problems. By the time Sherman had made his dispositions, it was probably too late for Hood to take Decatur as a crossing point without unacceptable losses from the reinforced garrison. A crossing point toward Tuscumbia was all but prohibited by the lack of enough supplies for the added distance back to Stevenson. In any case, enemy dispositions and intentions had very little influence on Hood and Beauregard at the time for the simple reason that they knew next to nothing about them.

Almost from the moment the army left Gadsden, Hood's communications with General Wheeler, his chief source of intelligence, started breaking down. The courier-telegraph line through Oxford, Selma, and Corinth was too slow and disjointed for its purpose, since it ended at Tuscumbia on the west. Couriers were required on both ends for Wheeler's telegraphic reports to reach the army. Reports by courier directly toward Decatur were understandably slow, but while the army was there they didn't reach Hood in time to matter. Hood wasn't sure where Sherman's army was or whether it was north or south of the river, and he didn't know of the movement of the Fourth Corps. On 2 November he hadn't heard from Wheeler for so long he thought the courier line had been broken by the enemy.[36]

Since 28 October Wheeler had reported consistently that Sherman was moving toward Atlanta, yet as late as 9 November Hood believed he had left three corps between Decatur Junction and Huntsville. On the thirteenth, General Beauregard advised Richmond that Sherman was moving toward Bridgeport with several corps. That day an exasperated Wheeler telegraphed Hood, "I did not say the Fifteenth and Seventeenth Corps were passing Bridgeport. They are still near Atlanta."[37] Wheeler was correct. Sherman had moved east to Rome on 28 October and further east to Kingston, Georgia, on 2 November, where he remained with one corps while his other two corps continued on to Smyrna Camp Grounds near

Atlanta. His army was "strung from Rome to Atlanta," as he put it.[38] He still thought Hood would be forced by public clamor to turn and follow him.[39]

These were the ramifications that made Hood pause at Decatur for four critical days, then change his campaign strategy. The notion of a quick dash to Stevenson was the whole thrust of his plan, and he clung doggedly to the idea of crossing the river at or near Decatur until the last moment. His aggressive demonstration on the twenty-eighth had earmarks of a last effort to bluff the fort into surrendering. The decision not to cross in this vicinity seems to have been a divided one, both among Hood's senior generals and between him and Beauregard. Only after they reached Courtland on the twenty-ninth did Hood finally admit to General Beauregard that too many of his men were without shoes, and he didn't have enough provisions to go into central Tennessee. There was nothing left to do but march to Tuscumbia where there was a good crossing place close to the railhead at Cherokee.[40]

At this juncture Beauregard began to fear they would never reach Nashville, and he said so to Hood, who then revealed his own despondence over the failure of his plan. Since they would be too far downstream to double back to Stevenson, Beauregard suggested instead that they begin a campaign directly through Middle Tennessee while most of the cavalry be sent to tear up the Nashville-Chattanooga Railroad. For lack of a better alternative Hood agreed. The next day, 30 October, the Army marched out of Courtland, and the bold scheme that had first motivated the Tennessee Campaign came to an end. After this, as Maj. D.W. Sanders,

Adjutant of French's Division, later wrote, "The lodgement of the army at Florence and Tuscumbia seemed a blind venture, the accident of circumstances that presented themselves, at different points, on the march from Gadsden, rather than the result of a matured plan of offensive operations."[41]

Most modern historians seem to agree with the assessment that Hood's plan for the Tennessee Campaign was "an impossible dream."[42] One says, "The difficulties and outright errors in such a plan were so profuse that the scheme would have made a text-book study at West Point."[43] Another calls it "probably the most poorly planned and executed major campaign of the war."[44] And another, "Hood's activities after Sherman left Atlanta [to follow Hood] seemed to have been scripted in never-never land."[45]

But many earlier writers gave Hood high marks for his initial plan to cut Sherman off at Stevenson and defeat General Thomas' scattered forces at Nashville. One source says, "Hood's scheme offered some chances of success if he moved fast enough and executed his plan effectively. The Federal forces in Tennessee were not united, being scattered instead all over the middle part of the state and vulnerable to defeat in detail."[46] General Beauregard, in his final report of the campaign, said quite positively that the original plan "would have led to the defeat of Thomas ... if executed without undue delay and modifications and with vigor and skill."[47] And Stanley F. Horn, a leading writer on the Army of Tennessee, said of the campaign, "If Hood had been able to move with just a little more celerity, if on just one or two occasions Fortune's balance had tilted in his favor instead of against him, his daringly conceived plan might well have succeeded and then perhaps the little village of Appomattox Court House might have slept forever in its dusty obscurity."[48]

This small action at Decatur was overshadowed by the tragic battles at Franklin and Nashville and has gone almost unnoticed in the history of the war, but the drastic change in his plan which took form there had profound implications for Hood in every aspect of the campaign. The abandonment of a river crossing near Stevenson was, in fact, a defining event that re-shaped the entire campaign. As Hood developed his plan for invading Tennessee in the week or so before it was finalized at the Gadsden meeting with Beauregard, there is not a hint that he envisioned an approach to Nashville by a long, slow march across Alabama. Had he foreseen this eventuality, it seems highly probable that he would have taken a different course of action (e.g. going into winter camp at Corinth or turning to follow Sherman), and there might not have been a Tennessee Campaign. In any case, once he settled on this alternative, the nature of the campaign changed in a fundamental way. Maneuver, grand tactics and speed of movement became almost irrelevant, and the campaign became a deliberate, head-on march to offer battle to a forewarned and reinforced enemy.

In the years since the war General Hood has been treated harshly by his critics. He has been faulted for lacking the administrative experience to command an army, for inadequate planning, being a poor logistician, not knowing how to use artillery, not making good use of reconnaissance and other things. Most of the grounds for these charges came together in the few days at and before the engagement at Decatur. This may explain the noticeable brevity of his recollection of the affair, as he later described the Tennessee Campaign. It is not mentioned in his official reports at the end of the campaign but is mentioned in his published memoirs.[49]

In his final report Hood says that on leaving Gadsden he hoped to cross the river at or near Guntersville, but "learning that Major General Forrest was not then in middle Tennessee, our march was continued to Tuscumbia, Alabama," giving the impression that he intended all along to move directly to Tuscumbia.[50] In his book *Advance and Retreat* he states, "I decided to deflect westward, effect a junction with Forrest and then cross the river at Florence .... The succeeding day the movement was continued toward Florence." In his only mention of the Decatur affair he describes it in one sentence: "While the Army turned Decatur, I ordered a slight demonstration to be made against the town till our forces passed safely beyond."[51] Given the importance of rapid movement to the success of his plan, this was not a credible explanation. Yet the implication that he spent four days using two army corps to neutralize the small fort while a third corps passed thirteen miles to the south has gone almost unchallenged. Based on what Confederate prisoners told him, General Granger expressed in his report a misinformed but, at the time, logical conclusion about Hood's intentions at Decatur. He wrote, "It is now positively known that the force opposed to us ... left Palmetto, Georgia, with the avowed intention of taking Decatur, as its occupation was deemed absolutely essential to them in their further offensive operations in Middle Tennessee."[51a]

Probably the first historiographer to question General Hood's intentions on the occasion wrote cautiously in 1875,

"His purpose in operating against Decatur has not been authentically revealed. All circumstances, except his own statement of his plan, lead to the belief that he expected to cross the Tennessee River at Decatur and move rapidly upon Sherman's communications in Middle Tennessee and cut off his supplies entirely."[52]

Colonel Doolittle was another who recognized the incongruity of General Hood's statement. As he wrote in 1890, "An army that moved with such celerity as his surely did not need four days to pass a place occupied by as small a force as we had the first day or two, especially the first day."[53] But these insights have been in the small minority, and the notion persisted for decades — and still does to a surprising degree — that Decatur was merely an impediment on the army's march to the west.

Many opinions have been advanced to rationalize General Hood's behavior at critical points in the campaign. One theory (without much standing) even suggests that his thinking was hampered at times by the laudanum he took for his pain. But there have been few explanations for his curious tactical direction of the fight at Decatur — the untimely and piecemeal nature of his attack, the minimum use of artillery, not breaking the pontoon bridge, leaving the Bridgeport bridge intact. To most people these lapses would be no mystery, considering the circumstances. Hood had detoured to Decatur on a spur-of-the moment decision with little or no planning, with insufficient or misleading intelligence information, and without the necessary logistical infrastructure. Under the extreme pressure of time and with his theatre commander looking over his shoulder and the president watching his movements closely from Richmond, he faced a convoluted set of circumstances that momentarily got out of control. The truth seems to be that he simply became rattled and confused. This would be understandable, perhaps even excusable, except that it played a part in the dissolution of a Confederate Army.[54]

CHAPTER NINE

Epilogue

FROM DECATUR THE ARMY MOVED TO TUSCUMBIA where it was delayed for three weeks while General Hood gathered supplies and waited for Forrest. Finally on 21 November it marched out on the Lawrenceburg, Chisolm and Waynesboro roads toward Columbia, Tennessee. There the Fourth and Twenty-third Corps under the command of General Schofield, still General Thomas' only infantry field force, arrived from Pulaski barely in time to set up a defense line. Hood ordered Lee's Corps to attack while he took Stewart's and Cheatham's Corps on a flanking move and passed behind Schofield to Spring Hill, cutting off the Union force. It was a brilliant maneuver which seemed a golden opportunity for Hood, but through a curious mix-up of orders, Schofield was allowed to march unopposed through Spring Hill that night within sight of Confederate camp fires and escape to Franklin. Hood was to write later, "The best move of my career as a soldier I was thus destined to behold come to naught."[1]

The next day, 30 November, he followed the Union force and hastily ordered an immediate infantry assault across open ground against Schofield's barricades at Franklin without waiting for Lee's Corps and the artillery to catch up. Standing on Winstead Hill overlooking Franklin, Hood turned to one of his corps commanders and quietly said, "General, we will make the fight."[2] On a hazy Indian Summer afternoon with bands playing on both sides, the army marched down the hill with parade-ground precision straight at the substantial breastworks left from an earlier occupation. By midnight the Army of Tennessee had been decimated in one of the war's bloodiest battles. The Union forces had been preparing to leave Franklin when the army attacked, and they left during the night after the battle. The battle seemed almost pointless, but it had been Hood's last chance to defeat Schofield before he could combine with Thomas' force. Confederate casualties were more than 6,200 men including sixty-four regiment and brigade commanders and a division commander. Six Confederate generals were killed or mortally wounded, five were wounded and one captured. Union losses were about 2,300.[3]

Schofield withdrew to Nashville during the night and joined General Thomas' force, which had finally been reinforced just the day before during the battle at Franklin by the two divisions from Missouri. Behind extensive fortifications Thomas could now muster nearly 50,000 men. With its strength reduced to 23,207 men, the Army of Tennessee followed and deployed in front of Nashville in some of the worst winter weather in years. Hood waited, unsure what to do next but hoping somehow for reinforcements from General Kirby Smith across the Mississippi River. Both armies were icebound by a winter storm for a week until 14 December when the weather moderated.[4]

On the fifteenth, Thomas attacked with his superior force, and the next day Hood's left flank caved in. The army was driven back in a disorderly retreat that continued to Bainbridge on the Tennessee River near Florence. Only the heroic rear-guard action of Forrest's cavalry and 1,900 men of Walthal's Division kept the Army from further destruction. Barely 15,000 men crossed the river to safety on 26 and 27 December. Of those who didn't return, 13,189 were captured, including seven generals, sixteen colonels and 1,000 other officers. A thousand men deserted and took the oath for the Union, but a great many men simply wandered away from the army and eventually went home, believing the cause was lost. The survivors left a ninety-mile path of bloody footprints on the icy, rutted roads from Nashville after suffering unbelievable hardships from the cold and lack of clothes and shoes.

"It stands without parallel in History. It was the roughest, the severest, the hardest and most desperate fighting, the saddest and most pitiable, the bloodiest and most disastrous of the war to the southern soldiers," said Charles Gore Joy of the Fourteenth Tennessee Cavalry, forty-seven years later. General Hood's message to Secretary of War Seddon on 3 January 1865 said, "The army has recrossed the Tennessee River without material loss since the battle in front of Nashville."[5]

At Bainbridge the pontoon bridge which had served the fort at Decatur so well played a small but vital role, this time for the Confederates. Under orders from General Thomas, the Union garrison had evacuated Decatur on 26 November after burning the fort's provisions and ammunition. Harried by an attack from the Fourth Alabama Cavalry under Lt. Col. F.M. Windes of Roddey's command, they left fifteen spare pontoons intact as gunboats and transports towed the bridge pontoons away. These fifteen pontoons became the center of attention later when the army had crossed the Duck River at

Columbia on its frantic retreat from Nashville, and it became questionable whether there would be enough pontoons to cross the Tennessee.[6]

General Hood took action to retrieve every pontoon that could be found. Two hundred men were sent to retrieve damaged boats abandoned along the roads. Capt. Robert L. Cobb of the Engineer Battalion and a company of pontoniers mounted on mules were sent to Decatur to float the fifteen boats there down the river. As engineers at Bainbridge tried to finish building a bridge and regiments arrived with sounds of battle coming ominously from their rear, Cobb and his men showed up with enough pontoons to complete the last gap in the bridging. They were cheered as saviors by crowds of men anxiously waiting to cross. As Col. Sumner A. Cunningham of the Forty-first Tennessee said, if they had waited on their own pontoons, "Bainbridge would have been noted in history as the place of surrender of Hood's army."[7]

General Hood resigned from his command on 10 January, and the remnants of the army were organized at Tupelo, Mississippi, by Lieutenant General Taylor, but they never again fought as an army. French's Division was sent to Mobile and was later captured at Spanish Fort seven miles east of Mobile and sent to prison camp at Ship Island. Other units were sent to Gen. Joseph E. Johnston's command in the east. The 5000 or so men who reached there fought at the Battle of Bentonville, North Carolina, before the final surrender of the Confederate armies in April 1865.[8]

On 27 December a Union force under Maj. Gen. James B. Steedman and General Granger landed from riverboats near Flint River, and by 6:00 p.m. reoccupied Decatur without opposition. It remained occupied for the rest of the war. Except for the Hinds-McEntire and Polk homes and the hotel and bank, there was nothing left of the town of Decatur. Every other building had been burned or torn down.[9]

Organization of the Army of Tennessee

General John B. Hood
C.S. Army Commanding, October 26, 1864

CHEATHAM'S CORPS — Maj. Gen. Benjamin F. Cheatham

BROWN'S DIVISION — Maj. Gen. John C. Brown
Gist's Bde. — Brig. Gen. States Rights Gist
46th, 65th Georgia; 2nd, 8th Georgia Battalions;
16th, 24th South Carolina
Maney's Bde. — Col. George C. Porter
1st, 6th, 9th, 19th, 27th, 34th, 46th, 50th Tennessee
Wright's Bde. — Brig. Gen John C. Carter*
8th, 16th, 28th, 38th, 51st, 53rd Tennessee
Strahl's Bde. — Brig. Gen. Otho F. Strahl
4th, 5th, 24th, 31st, 33rd, 41st Tennessee
Vaughn's Bde. — Brig. Gen. George W. Gordon
11th, 12th, 13th, 29th, 47th, 154th Tennessee

CLEBURNE'S DIVISION — Maj. Gen. Patrick R. Cleburne
Lowrey's Bde. — Brig. Gen. Mark P. Lowrey
16th, 33rd, 45th Alabama; 3rd Mississippi Battalion;
5th, 8th, 32nd Mississippi
Govan's Bde. — Col. Peter V. Green
1st, 2nd, 5th, 6th, 7th, 8th, 13th, 15th, 19th, 24th
Arkansas; 3rd Confederate
Granbury's Bde. — Brig. Gen. Hiram B. Granbury
5th Confederate; 35th Tennessee; 6th, 7th, 10th Texas;
15th, 17th, 18th, 24th, 25th Texas Cavalry (dismounted);
Louisiana Cavalry Company (dismounted)
Mercer's Bde. — Col. Charles H. Olmstead**
1st Volunteer Georgia; 54th, 57th, 63rd Georgia

BATE'S DIVISION — Maj. Gen. William B. Bate
 Tyler's Bde. — Brig. Gen. Thomas B. Smith
  37th Georgia; 4th Ga. Battalion Sharpshooters;
  2nd Tennessee (Provisional Army);
  10th, 15th, 20th, 30th, 37th Tennessee
 Finley's Bde. — Col. Robert Bullock
  1st, 3rd, 4th, 6th, 7th Florida; 1st Florida Cavalry
  (dismounted)
 Jackson's Bde. — Col. William D. Mitchell
  1st Georgia (Confederate); 1st Georgia Battalion
  Sharpshooters; 25th, 29th, 30th, 66th Georgia

STEWART'S CORPS — Lieut. Gen. Alexander P. Stewart

LORING'S DIVISION — Maj. Gen. William W. Loring
 Featherston's Bde. — Brig. Gen. Winfield S. Featherston
  1st, 3rd, 22nd, 31st, 33rd, 40th Mississippi;
  1st Mississippi Battalion Sharpshooters
 Adams' Bde. — Brig. Gen. John Adams
  6th, 14th, 15th, 20th, 23rd, 43rd Mississippi
 Scott's Bde. — Brig. Gen. Thomas M. Scott
  27th, 35th, 49th, 55th, 57th, Alabama; 12th Louisiana

FRENCH'S DIVISION — Maj. Gen. Samuel G. French
 Ector's Bde. — Brig. Gen. William H. Young
  29th, 39th North Carolina; 9th Texas;
  10th, 14th, 32nd Texas Cavalry (dismounted)
 First Missouri Bde. — Brig. Gen. Francis M. Cockrell
  1st, 2nd, 3rd, 4th, 5th, 6th Missouri;
  1st, 3rd Missouri Cavalry (dismounted)
 Sears' Bde. — Brig. Gen. Claudius W. Sears
  4th, 35th, 36th, 39th, 46th Mississippi;
  7th Mississippi Battalion

WALTHAL'S DIVISION — Maj. Gen. Edward C. Walthal
Quarles' Bde. — Brig. Gen. William R. Quarles
   1st Alabama; 42nd, 46th, 48th, 49th, 53rd, 55th Tennessee
Cantey's Bde. — Col. Edward A. O'Neal
   17th, 26th, 29th Alabama; 37th Mississippi
Reynolds' Bde. — Brig. Gen. Daniel H. Reynolds
   1st, 2nd Arkansas Mounted Rifles (dismounted);
   4th, 9th, 25th Arkansas

LEE'S CORPS — Lt. Gen. Stephen D. Lee (bypassed Decatur)

CAVALRY CORPS — Maj. Gen. Joseph Wheeler (detached to
  guard flank)

JACKSON'S CAVALRY DIVISION — Brig. Gen. William H. Jackson
Armstrong's Bde. — Brig. Gen. Frank C. Armstrong
   1st, 2nd, 28th Mississippi; Ballentine's Mississippi
Ross' Bde. — Brig. Gen. Lawrence S. Ross
   3rd, 6th, 9th, 27th Texas
Ferguson's Bde. — Col. William Boyles (detached to
  Wheeler's Corps)
Lewis' Bde. — Brig. Gen. Joseph H. Lewis (detached to
  Wheeler's Corps)

ARTILLERY
Maj. Gen. Arnold Elzey

CHEATHAM'S CORPS — Col. Melancton Smith

Hoxton's Battalion — Capt. William B. Turner
   Marion (Florida) Light Artillery Battery; Phelan's
   Alabama Battery; Turner's Mississippi Battery

Hotchkiss' Battalion — Capt. Hiram M. Bledsoe
*Goldthwaite's Alabama Battery; Key's Arkansas Battery;
Bledsoe's Missouri Battery*
Cobb's Battalion — Maj. Robert Cobb
*Ferguson's South Carolina Battery;
Mebane's Tennessee Battery;
5th Company, Washington Light Artillery (Louisiana)*

STEWART'S CORPS — Lt. Col. Samuel C. Williams

Trueheart's Battalion — Maj. Daniel Trueheart
*Tarrant's Alabama, Selden's Alabama, Lumsden's Alabama
Batteries*
Myrick's Battalion — Maj. John D. Myrick
*Cowan's Mississippi, Darden's Mississippi Batteries;
Point Coupee (Louisiana) Artillery*
Storrs' Battalion — Maj. George S. Storrs
*Haskins' Mississippi, Guibor's Missouri, Kolb's Alabama
Batteries*

HORSE ARTILLERY

JACKSON'S DIVISION — Capt. John Waties
*Clark's Missouri Battery; Columbus (Georgia) Artillery;
Waties' South Carolina Battery*

* Brigade dissolved and regiments reassigned to other brigades by 20 November.
** Commander changed to Brig. Gen. James A. Smith on 20 November return.

Sources: OR 39, 2, 851-859; OR 45, 1, 665-668; OR 45, 1, 678-682; McDonough, *Five Tragic Hours,* 200-207.

Fords and Ferries on the Tennessee River
Between Chattanooga and Florence

Fords and Ferries	Character/Condition	Miles	Remarks
City of Chattanooga			
Ross Tow-Head		3	Island
Ross Shoals	Fordable	3	High land on north side and flat on south; approaches not good
Mouth of Chattanooga Creek		4	South side
Mouth of Lookout Creek		5	South side
Brown's Ferry	Not used	9	
William's Island		10	Island 2 miles long, farm on north side
Tumbling Shoals		13	
The Suck Boiling Pot Skillet The Pan	Warp at ordinary stage Warp only at high water Warp only at low water Warp only at high water	19	River is narrow between the mountains. At these points boatmen are obliged to warp their vessels past
Kelley's Ferry	Very good ferry; flatboats	29	Road from Jasper to Chattanooga; approaches good
Colonel Hall's Farm		37	
Running Water Creek		40	
Rankin's Ferry	Good ferry; flatboats	41	Rankin's farm on north side; approaches good
Shellmound Depot		45	South side one-half mile to mountains; north side bluff
Mouth of Sequatchie River		49	
Lowry's Ferry, Long Island	Very good ferry	52	South side level; north side hilly; approaches good

Fords and Ferries	Character/Condition	Miles	Remarks
Mouth of Battle Creek		53	North side
Town of Bridgeport, Long Island		58	
Mouth of Island Creek		62	South side
Widow's Shoals	Good ford	65	Mouth of Widow's Creek, north side of Sand Mountain come up to the river; approaches good
Caperton's Ferry	Flat row-boat; good	73	Nearly south from Stevenson; the road crossing this ferry is said to be the nearest south from Stevenson across Sand Mountain
Crow Creek, Crow Island		77	North side
Caperton's Ford	Very good ford	80	Much used at ordinary low state; approaches good
Bellefonte Island		86	Mountains near the river for 3 or 4 miles
Bellefonte Creek		86	Five miles to mountains. North side
Bellefonte Landing		89	Three miles to Bellefonte, county seat of Jackson County
Bellefonte Shoals	Good ford	90	No road crossing; Sand Mountains close to river; approaches bad
Mouth of Crow Creek		93	South side
Larkin's Landing, Larkin's Ferry	Good and much used	105	Highlands north side; three-quarters of a mile to Sand Mountain; approaches good
Mouth of Santa Creek		117	North side
Pine Island		119	Three miles long; South Santa Creek
Center Island			South side

Fords and Ferries	Character/Condition	Miles	Remarks
Buck Island		129	Fine country intervening these islands
Gunter's Shoals, Gunter's Island		133	Five miles long
Gunter's Landing		138	
Old Deposit Ferry	Good ferry; row-boats	145	South side low, flat country; north side bluffs; approaches good
Mouth of Paint Rock River		159	North side
Flint Tow Head		163	Mouth of Flint River
Whitesburg or Huntsville Landing, Whitesburg		168	Good pike to Huntsville
Butler's Ferry	Good ferry	173	Much used; approaches good
Massey's Ferry	Country ferry	176	Not much used
Town of Triana		184	Mouth of Indian Creek (north side)
Fletcher's Ferry	Flat-boat; good	188	Approaches good
Mouth of Linestone Creek		193	
Mouth of Flint Creek		196	South side
Town of Decatur		199	
Brown's Island		210	Three miles long
Brown's Ferry	Horse-boat; good	217	Road crossing from Athens to Courtland; approaches good
Mouth of Elk River		229	North side
Lamb's Ferry	Good ferry	232	Approaches good
Head of Muscle Shoals		233	About 20 miles long; the most difficult of passing on the river
Town of Florence		252	
Tuscumbia Landing		260	

Source: OR Series 1, Vol. 30, Part 3, 266-267. Undated (about 31 August 1863).

APPENDIX C

Evacuation Order

Headquarters Left Wing, Sixteenth Army Corps
Athens, Ala., March 19, 1864

Brig. Gen. JOHN D. STEVENSON,
Commanding Detachment Fourth Division, Decatur:

    I inclose an order that no doubt will cause some hardships. When persons desire to go north and are poor people, you can give them transportation by railroad. If you have any unserviceable, worn out stock, you can let families have a team where they have no other means of moving. Take particular pains that nothing is destroyed and that all property left is got together and stored with some responsible party.

    We desire to cover all movements, and therefore be very strict with your picket lines and allow no person to come in unless he is a refugee to join our army or a negro whom we can use to advantage except when in your judgement you can obtain some information that is to our advantage that all these people should move as far south or north as possible.

    I am, very respectfully, your obedient servant.

        G.M. DODGE, *Brigadier-General, Commanding*

[inclosure]

SPECIAL ORDERS } *Hdqrs. Left Wing, 16th Army Corps,*
No. 72   } *Athens, Ala., March 19, 1864*

I. *The necessities of the army require the use of every building in Decatur for Government purposes. It is therefore ordered:*

    First. That all citizens living in Decatur or within 1 mile of the limits of the town on the south side of the Tennessee River shall move outside of the lines within six days from the receipt of this order.

    Second. They will be allowed to go north or south, as they deem best, and take with them all their personal and movable property.

    Third. As fast as the buildings are vacated the commander of the post will take possession of them and see that they are preserved and no damage done to them.

    Fourth. No exception to this order will be made except in the case of families or persons of our army or employees of the Government.

    Fifth. Brig. Gen. J.D. Stevenson will cause this order to be immediately complied with.

    By order of Brig. Gen. G.M. Dodge:

        J.W. BARNES, *Assistant Adjutant-General*

Source: OR Series 1, Vol. 32, Part 3, 94-95.

NOTES

Chapter One. Prelude — Fall of Atlanta

1. Wolseley, "English View," 719. Wolseley added that he doubted if Hood could have taken the army through the mountains to attack Grant.
2. Henderson, *Science of War*, 235.
3. U.S. Government Printing Office. *The War of the Rebellion: A Compilation of the Official Records of the Union and Confederate Armies, 1861-1865,* Series I, vol. 32, part 3, 95, 122, 429. (Referred to hereafter as OR. All references are in series I. Only volume, part and page will be cited.)
4. OR 32, 3, 245-46.
5. Dyer, *Gallant Hood,* 20, 309.
6. McWhiney, *Southerners and Other Americans,* 121; McMurry, *Rise to Glory,* 45; Connally, *Autumn of Glory,* 433.
7. OR 38, 5, 777.
7a. Bailey, *Battles for Atlanta,* 136.
8. Vandiver, "General Hood as Logistician," 145; Coulter, *Confederate States of America,* 449; OR 38, 5, 1027.
9. Manigault, *Carolinian Goes to War,* 278.
10. Donovan, et al, eds. *American Civil War,* 218.
11. OR 39, 2, 880: Hood, *Advance and Retreat,* 253-255; Connally, *Politics of Command,* 164; Donovan, et al, eds. *American Civil War,* 218.
12. Roman, *Military Operations of General Beauregard,* 2: 292, 299; Cox, *Battle of Franklin,* 3; OR 38, 1, 27; *Memoirs of General William T. Sherman,* 2:141.

Chapter Two. Hood Turns North

1. *Memoirs of General William T. Sherman,* 2:144; OR 39, 1, 802; OR 39, 3, 390.
2. OR 39, 1, 585, 588; Van Horne, *Life of Major General Thomas,* 263; *Memoirs of General William T. Sherman,* 2:162.
3. Stone, "Battle of Franklin," 7:436.
4. Ibid., 442.
5. OR 39, 1, 590; *Memoirs of General William T. Sherman,* 2:162; VanHorne, *Life of Major General Thomas,* 264-265; Horne, *Army of Tennessee,* 381; OR 45, 1, 32-33.

166 *Detour to Disaster*

6. Boatner, *Civil War Dictionary,* 352; Warner, *Generals in Blue,* 182.
7. OR 39, 3, 154, 215; Mercur, *Attack of Fortified Places,* 99.
8. OR 49, 2, 978; Doolittle, "Defense of Decatur," 3:266.
9. OR 39, 1, 696.
10. Doolittle, "Defense of Decatur," 3:265.
11. OR 39, 3, 155.
12. OR 39, 3, 804; Hood, *Advance and Retreat,* 259-260.
13. OR 39, 3, 216.
14. OR 39, 3, 278, 318.
15. Dunnavant, *Decatur. Alabama: Yankee Foothold,* 111; Gibbons, *Warships and Naval Battles,* 163; U.S. Navy, *Civil War Chronology,* V-56; U.S. Government Printing Office. *Official Records of the Union and Confederate Navies in the War of the Rebellion,* Series 1, vol. 26: 573, 593, 731. (Referred to hereafter as ONR. All references are in series 1. Only volume and page will be cited.)
16. Lyon, *Reminiscences,* 173; Chadick, "Civil War Days," 261.
17. OR 39, 3, 805; Jones, *Gentle Rebel,* 102; Daniel, *Cannoneers in Gray,* 170.
18. Hood, *Advance and Retreat,* 256, 262; *Memoirs of General William T. Sherman,* 2:146; French, *Two Wars,* 264; OR 39, 1, 802, 812; 6-5, 671-672.
19. OR 39, 3, 155.
20. OR 39, 3, 333; *Memoirs of General William T. Sherman,* 2:153, 157.
21. OR 39, 3, 342.
22. OR 39, 3, 358.
23. *Memoirs of General William T. Sherman,* 2:157.
24. OR 39, 3, 358.

Chapter Three. Tennessee Campaign Strategy

1. Hood, *Advance and Retreat,* 264-268; Roman, *Military Operations of General Beauregard,* 2:287.
2. Hood, *Advance and Retreat,* 266-268; Roman, *Military Operations of General Beauregard,* 2:288; Hood, "Invasion of Tennessee," 4:427.
3. Dyer, *The Gallant Hood,* 271.
4. OR 45, 1, 647; Roman, *Military Operations of General Beauregard,* 2:288.
5. Roman, *Military Operations of General Beauregard* 2:287-288; Hood, *Advance and Retreat,* 268; Horn, *Army of Tennessee,* 379.
6. ____. *Military Operations of General Beauregard,* 2:291; Hood, *Advance and Retreat,* 269; Connally, *Autumn of Glory,* 435.

7. ____. *Military Operations of General Beauregard*, 2:285-286; Connally, *Autumn of Glory*, 485; OR 39, 1, 507; OR 39, 3, 837.
8. ____. *Military Operations of General Beauregard*, 2:285.
9. Hood, *Advance and Retreat*, 269; Whiteside, "Life of Lawrence Sullivan Ross," 48; OR 39, 3, 842; OR 38, 5, 1026.
10. Brown, *One of Cleburne's Command*, 153; Brewer, "Incidents of the Retreat from Nashville," 329; Mitchell, "Letters of a Confederate Surgeon," 174; Nelson, "Tennessee, a Grave or a Free Home," 508.
11. Vandiver, *Plowshares and Swords*, 221; Daniel, *Cannoneers in Gray*, 166; Gibbon, *Artillerist's Manual*, 391; Vandiver, "Hood as Logistician," 148; Ripley, *Artillery and Ammunition*, 196, 228; OR 45, 1, 334; OR 39, 2, 865.
12. DuBose, *General Joseph Wheeler and the Army of Tennessee*, 164; O'Connor, *Hood, Cavalier General*, 225; French, *Two Wars*, 287-288.
13. Horn, *Battle of Nashville*, 175-181; O'Connor, *Hood, Cavalier General*, 225.
14. *Personal Memoirs of Gen. D.S. Stanley*, 190; Van Horne, *Army of the Cumberland*, 2:167; *Memoirs of General William T. Sherman*, 2:159; OR 39, 3, 395, 436.
15. *Personal Memoirs of Gen. D.S. Stanley*, 189.
16. Ibid., 189, 197.
17. Hood, *Advance and Retreat*, 225; Woodworth, *Jefferson Davis and His Generals*, 189; OR, 38, 5, 893; OR 52, 2, 745.
18. Bailey, *Battles for Atlanta*, 90; Daniel, *Cannoneers in Gray*, 169; OR 39, 2, 857.
19. OR 39, 3, 837, 841.
20. OR 39, 3, 841, 842.
21. OR 39, 3, 837, 841; Hood, *Advance and Retreat*, 268, 270.
22. OR 39, 3, 845.
23. Ibid.
24. OR 39, 1, 797; OR 39, 3, 329; McMurry, *John Bell Hood and the War*, 163.
25. OR 39, 3, 845; OR 52, 2, 767; Plum, *Military Telegraph*, 208.
26. Graham, Diary; OR 39, 3, 842.
27. OR 39, 1, 803; OR 39, 3, 913; Hood, *Advance and Retreat*, 270; Roman, *Military Operations of General Beauregard*, 2: 293.
28. OR 39, 3, 448; Connally, *Autumn of Glory*, 486; Hay, *Hood's Tennessee Campaign*, 58; Horn, *Army of Tennessee*, 380.
29. Lindsley, *Military Annals of Tennessee*, 300, 829.

30. OR 39, 1, 588.
31. OR 39, 1, 807; Graham, Diary; Jones, *Civil War in Decatur,* 2.
32. Taylor, *Reluctant Rebel,* 25.
33. Ibid., 241.
34. Lossen, *Tennessee's Forgotten Warriors,* 166; Lindsley, Military *Annals of Tennessee,* 300.
35. Horn, *Army of Tennessee,* 421; Graham, Diary; Coggins, *Arms and Equipment,* 17; Thompson, *E.M. Graham,* 22, 95-96n.
36. OR 39, 3, 431-432, 436, 448-449; Horn, *Army of Tennessee,* 381; *Memoirs of General William T. Sherman,* 2:161.
37. OR 39, 3, 433.
38. OR 39, 1, 695; OR 39, 3, 436.
39. OR 39, 3, 154; Doolittle, "Defense of Decatur," 3:265-266; Reid, *Ohio in the War,* 2:554; Robertson, *Michigan in the War,* 306; Wisconsin Adjutant General, *Annual Report,* 223.
40. Andes and McTeer, *Loyal Mountain Troopers,* vi, x, 163.
41. Ohio General Assembly, *Official Roster,* 479; Elliott, *Transport to Disaster,* 214; Berry, *Loss of the Sultana,* 395-397.

Chapter Four. Testing Decatur Defenses

1. OR 39, 1, 807; OR 39, 3, 852; Goodloe, *Confederate Echoes,* 229. Jones, *Civil War in Decatur,* 11.
2. OR 39, 1, 807; Hood, *Advance and Retreat,* 271; Brewer, *Alabama: Her History,* 495; Dunnavant, *Decatur: Yankee Foothold,* 121.
2a. Williams to Gale, After-Action Report; Tarrant to Gale, After-Action Report.
3. OR 39, 3, 491; Goodloe, *Confederate Echoes,* 18, 230-231; Andes and McTeer, *Loyal Mountain Troopers,* 163.
4. OR 39, 1, 700; Doolittle, "Defense of Decatur," 3:267; Andes and McTeer, *Loyal Mountain Troopers,* 163; *Autobiography of Major Will A. McTeer,* 98.
5. Goodloe, *Confederate Echoes,* 230-231; Graham, Diary; Noyes, "Excerpts from the Diary of E.T. Eggleston," 353.
5a. Darden to Mason, After-Action Report.
6. Confederate States of America Papers, Service Record Abstracts; French, *Two Wars,* 288.
7. Miller, *Forgotten Regiment,* 187, 188, 213.
8. Robertson, *Michigan in the War,* 387, 482-483; OR 39, 1, 701.
9. OR 39, 1, 701, 704, 712; Doolittle, "Defense of Decatur," 3:267; Schmutz, *History of 102d Ohio,* 171.

10. OR 39, 1, 701.
11. Ibid.; Andes and McTeer, *Loyal Mountain Troopers,* 164.
12. OR 39, 1, 704.
13. Andes and McTeer, *Loyal Mountain Troopers,* 164; *Autobiography of Major Will A. McTeer,* 99; Doolittle, "Defense of Decatur," 3:270.
14. OR 39, 1, 707; Andes and McTeer, *Loyal Mountain Troopers,* 165.
15. OR 39, 1, 707; Tennessee, Adjutant General, *Report,* 332-349; Doolittle, "Defense of Decatur," 3:270; Andes and McTeer, *Loyal Mountain Troopers,* 165.
16. OR 39, 1, 701, 713; Doolittle, "Defense of Decatur" 3:267-268.
17. OR 39, 1, 705-706; Ohio General Assembly, *Official Roster,* 495; Tennessee Adjutant General, *Report,* 654; Doolittle, "Defense of Decatur" 3:210; Schmutz, *History of 102d Ohio,* 171-172. Captain Cooper mistakenly identified the guns he ordered to the left of the parapet as the remaining section of Captain Beach's battery, but this section was on temporary duty at Athens. It returned to the fort at 2:30 a.m. on the 28th and was placed on the right flank.
18. OR 39, 1, 701; Jones, *Civil War in Decatur,* 8; OR 39, 3, 452.
18a. Darden to Mason, 1 Nov 64; Haskins, After-Action Report.
18b. Haskins, After-Action Report; Tarrant to Gale, After-Action Report; Darden to Mason, After-Action Report; Eggleston, "Scenes Where General Tilghman was Killed," 196.
19. Lyon, *Reminiscences,* 173n.
20. Ibid.
21. OR 39, 3, 451.
22. OR 39, 3, 452.
23. Ibid.
24. OR 39, 1, 696.
25. OR 39, 1, 701; Goodloe, *Confederate Echoes,* 230; Last Roll, *Confederate Veteran,* 13 (September 1905) 424; Wheeler, *Alabama,* 167; Brewer, *Alabama, Her History,* 644; Noyes, "Excerpts from the Diary of E.T. Eggleston," 353.
26. Collins, "Sad Story," 116; Sykes, Columbus. Papers; Jones, *Gentle Rebel,* 103, 131. William E. Sykes was born of George Augustus and Mary Edmund Sykes in 1838. Edward T. Sykes was born of Richard and Martha Sykes in the same year.
27. Miller, *Recollections of a Pine Knot,* 20.
28. Yeary, *Reminiscences,* 705, 795.
29. Smith, *Company F, First Alabama,* 112.
30. Zorn, *Hold at All Hazards,* 110.

31. Bevens, *Reminiscences of a Private,* 203.
32. Lavender, *They Never Came Back,* 104-106.
33. Ibid.
34. Graham, Diary.
35. OR 39, 1, 471.
36. Doolittle, "Defense of Decatur" 3:273; Taylor, *Reluctant Rebel,* 241; Smith, *Company F, First Alabama,* 113-115.
37. Tower, *A Carolinian Goes to War,* 277; Mitchell, "Letters of a Confederate Surgeon," 174.
38. Roundtree, "Letters From a Confederate Soldier," 296.
39. Ibid., 297; Tower, *A Carolinian Goes to War,* 277.
40. OR 39, 1, 701, 713; Coggins, *Arms and Equipment,* 62; Schmutz, *History of the 102d Ohio,* 171; *History of the Seventy-third Indiana,* 195.
41. OR 39, 1, 696, 709.
42. Chadick, "Civil War Days in Huntsville," 280.
43. OR 39, 1, 711; Jones, *Civil War in Decatur,* 10.
44. OR 39, 3, 853.
45. OR 39, 1, 605; OR 39, 3, 446, 853.
46. Sanders, "Hood's Tennessee Campaign" 3:245-246.
47. OR 39, 3, 449.
48. OR 39, 1, 605; *Memoirs of General William T. Sherman,* 2:161-162; Hay, *Hood's Tennessee Campaign,* 47.

Chapter Five. Vacillation, Fort Reinforced

1. OR 39, 3, 469, 471.
2. OR 39, 3, 470; Andes and McTeer, *Loyal Mountain Troopers,* 165-166; *Autobiography of Major Will A. McTeer,* 100-101.
3. OR 39, 3, 470.
4. OR 39, 1, 588, 696, 709; *History of the Seventy-Third Indiana,* 98, 104; Jones, *Civil War in Decatur,* 14.
5. Jones, *Civil War in Decatur,* 16; OR 39, 1, 714; Morgan, *Reminiscences of Service,* 11-32, 35; Berlin, *Black Military Experience,* 556; Williams, *History of the Negro Troops,* 274-275.
6. Romeyn, "With Colored Troops in the Army," 65.
7. Collins, "Sad Story of the War," 116; Sykes, Columbus. Papers.
8. Jones, *Gentle Rebel,* 103.
9. Smith, *Company F, First Alabama,* ii, 112-113.
9a. Crumpton, *Book of Memories,* 93-94.
10. Worsham, *Old Nineteenth Tennessee,* 136, 148.
11. Shannon, "Sharpshooters with Hood's Army," 123.

11a. Darden to Mason, After-Action Report; Haskins, After-Action Report; Harris to Storrs, After-Action Report.

12. OR 45, 1, 735; Graham, Diary; Daniel, *Soldiering in the Army of Tennessee,* 156; French, *Two Wars,* 288.

13. OR 52, 2, 769; Roman, *Military Operations of General Beauregard,* 2:292.

14. Roman, *Military Operations of General Beauregard,* 2:293. Roman's book was written largely from notes and papers authenticated by General Beauregard and is considered to be essentially autobiographical. Beauregard's actual words were probably more earthy than this but may have been edited to this form by him.

15. OR 45, 1, 648; Connally, *Autumn of Glory,* 486; Roman, *Military Operations of General Beauregard,* 2:293.

16. OR 39, 1, 697; Andes and McTeer, *Loyal Mountain Troopers,* 169.

17. Andes and McTeer, *Loyal Mountain Troopers,* 171.

18. OR 39, 1, 697, 716; *Autobiography of Major Will A. McTeer,* 101.

19. OR 39, 1, 697, 716; Andes and McTeer, *Loyal Mountain Troopers,* 166; Romeyn, *With Colored Troops,* 65.

20. Andes and McTeer, *Loyal Mountain Troopers,* 166; OR 39, 1, 697, 716.

21. OR 39, 1, 588, 709; OR 49, 2, 978; High, *History of the 68th Indiana,* 188.

22. OR 39, 3, 467, 471, 855; Van Horne, *History of the Army of the Cumberland,* 2:265.

23. Palfrey, "General Sherman's Plans," 512.

Chapter Six. Counterattack Stalls Demonstration

1. OR 39, 1, 696, 697.

2. OR 39, 1, 696, 827; Jones, *Civil War in Decatur,* 19; Doolittle, "Defense of Decatur" 3:271.

3. OR 39, 1, 696; Andes and McTeer, *Loyal Mountain Troopers,* 167.

4. OR 39, 1, 696; Doolittle, "Defense of Decatur" 3:271; Jenkins, *Story of Decatur,* 122.

5. OR 39, 1, 696-697, 709, 712; Andes and McTeer, *Loyal Mountain Troopers,* 168; *Autobiography of Major Will A. McTeer,* 100.

6. Andes and McTeer, *Loyal Mountain Troopers,* 168; *Autobiography of Major Will A. McTeer,* 101; Knox, *History of Morgan County,* 187.

7. OR 39, 1, 708, 709, 711, 712.

8. Andes and McTeer, *Loyal Mountain Troopers,* 168; *Autobiography of Major Will A. McTeer,* 101.

9. OR 39, 1, 708.
10. OR 39, 1, 697; OR 39, 3, 488; *Autobiography of Major Will A. McTeer,* 100.
11. OR 39, 3, 488.
12. Ibid.
13. OR 39, 1, 827.
14. Henderson, *Roster of Confederate Soldiers of Georgia,* 4:23ff; Ibid. 6:696ff; Cooper, *Civil War Diary,* 166.
15. Henderson, *Roster of Confederate Soldiers of Georgia,* 3:498ff; Adamson, *Brief History of the Thirtieth Georgia,* 70ff.
16. OR 39, 1, 710; Robertson, *Michigan in the War,* 218-219, 235; Auer, "Queen of Texas Ghost Towns," 126-128. Indianola was then the most important seaport and supply center on the Texas coast. It was the U.S. Army Quartermaster depot for the Department of Texas, supplying the frontier forts in Texas, as well as a commercial port for cattle, freight and passengers. The town was largely destroyed by a hurricane in 1875, then destroyed by an even stronger hurricane in 1886. Today there is nothing left of the town, but it still shows on a few maps near Port Lavaca on Matagorda Bay.
16a. Williams to Gale, After-Action Report.
17. Romeyn, "With Colored Troops," 66.
18. OR 39, 1, 697, 716; Morgan "Reminiscences of Service with Colored Troops," 534.
19. OR 39, 1, 717.
19a. Noyes, "Excerpts from the Civil War Diary of E.T. Eggleston," 339.
20. Romeyn, "With Colored Troops," 66.
20a. Darden to Mason, After-Action Report.
21. OR 39, 1, 698.
22. OR 39, 1, 698, 714-715.
23. Ibid.
24. Romeyn, "With Colored Troops," 66.
25. OR 39, 1, 714-715.
26. Graham, Diary; Williams, *History of Negro Troops,* 280; Romeyn, "With Colored Troops," 66; OR 39, 1, 714-715; Andes and McTeer, *Loyal Mountain Troopers,* 169-170.
26a. OR 39, 1, 715.
27. OR 39, 1, 709-710; Jones, *Gentle Rebel,* 104; Andes and McTeer, *Loyal Mountain Troopers,* 170; Graham, Diary; Jones, *Civil War in Decatur,* 24.
28. OR 39, 1, 715; OR 39, 3, 488; Jones, *Civil War in Decatur,* 24.

28a. Romeyn, "With Colored Troops," 66.

29. OR 39, 1, 716; Morgan, "Reminiscences of Service," 36.

29a. Haskins, After-Action Report; Tarrant, Darden to Gale,
     After-Action Report, Pat to Mason, After-Action Report; Last Roll,
     Confederate Veteran, 22 (June 1910) 280.

30. French, *Two Wars,* 288; Haskins, After-Action Report; Tarrant to
    Gale, After-Action Report.

31. OR 39, 3, 488.

32. Reid, *Ohio in the War,* 2:707; Robertson, *Michigan in the War,* 235.
    Both the Third and Fourth Michigan regiments had fought in the
    battles around Virginia until the expiration of their terms of enlist-
    ment, then re-formed with new men on a nucleus of veterans.

33. Gay, *Life in Dixie,* 247.

34. Ibid., 247, 262; Andes and McTeer, *Loyal Mountain Troopers,* 167;
    OR 39, 1, 711.

35. Brown, *One of Cleburne's Command,* 142.

36. Cunningham, *Reminiscences,* 36.

37. Nelson, "Tennessee, A Grave or a Free Home," 508; Rennolds,
    History of the Henry County Commands, 102; Graham, Diary; Jones,
    Civil War in Decatur, 13.

38. ONR 26, 592; OR 39, 1, 698.

39. Eggleston, "Excerpts From the Civil War Diary," 353; Kolb to Gale,
    After-Action Report

40. OR 39, 1, 698; Andes and McTeer, *Loyal Mountain Troopers,* 169;
    McTeer, *Autobiography,* 102.

41. Darden to Mason, After-Action Report; Tarrant to Gale, After-
    Action Report; Haskins, After-Action Report; ONR 26, 593, 598;
    OR 39, 1, 648.

42. OR 39, 1, 717; Darden to Mason, After-Action Report.

43. Andes and McTeer, *Loyal Mountain Troopers,* 169.

44. OR 39, 1, 648; OR 39, 3, 503.

45. OR 39, 1, 705, 710, 717; Indiana, Adjutant General, *Report,* 697.

46. Last Roll, *Confederate Veteran,* 22 (June 1910) 280; Nevin, *Civil
    War,* 33; Rowland, *Military History of Mississippi,* 482; Yeary,
    Reminiscences, 795.

47. Jones, *Gentle Rebel,* 104.

48. Ibid., ix.

49. Chadick, "Civil War Days," 281.

50. OR 39, 1, 715.

51. ONR, 26:593-594.

52. OR 39, 3, 859; Dodson, *Campaigns of Wheeler,* 277.
53. OR 39, 1, 589; OR 39, 3, 859, 863, 879; OR 52, 2, 770.
54. OR 39, 3, 858, 865, 522; Foote, *The Civil War,* 3:628, 289; Roman, *Military Operations of General Beauregard,* 2:293-294; Van Horne, *History of the Army of the Cumberland,* 120.
55. OR 39, 3, 858.
56. OR 39, 3, 477; Stone, "Battle of Franklin" 7:441; *Memoirs of General William T. Sherman,* 2:371; Fisk, *Mississippi Valley in the War,* 333.
57. OR 39, 3, 477-478, 484, 485; Stone, "Battle of Franklin" 7:521.

Chapter Seven. Counting Railroad Ties Toward Tuscumbia

1. OR 39, 3, 704-705; Doolittle, "Defense of Decatur" 3:273.
2. OR 39, 1, 710, 715; Morgan, "Reminiscences of Service," 35-36.
3. OR 39, 3, 504-506.
4. OR 39, 3, 865-866; Bevens, *Reminiscences,* 203-205; French, *Two Wars,* 289; Graham, Diary.
4a. French, *Two Wars,* 289.
4b. Cunningham, *Reminiscences of the Forty-first Tennessee,* 36.
5. OR 45, 1, 767-768; Brewer, *Alabama, Her History,* 704; *Autobiography of James Robert Maxwell,* 237, 258.
6. Andes and McTeer, *Loyal Mountain Troopers,* 170; *Autobiography of Major Will A. McTeer,* 103.
7. OR 39, 1, 699, 702; Doolittle, "Defense of Decatur" 3:272.
8. OR 39, 1, 589; OR 39, 3, 865-866; OR 45, 1, 572.
9. OR 39, 1, 696; OR 39, 3, 506.
10. OR 39, 1, 699; OR 39, 3, 522-523.
11. OR 39, 1, 812.
12. Ibid., 826.
13. Van Horn, *History of the Army of the Cumberland,* 2:168.
14. Lonn, *Desertion During the Civil War,* 78; OR 32, 3, 284.
15. Andes and McTeer, *Loyal Mountain Troopers,* 172; Daniel, *Soldiering in the Army of Tennessee,* 164.
16. Jones, "Roster of Medical Officers," 266; Steryx, ed. "Autobiography and Letters of Joel Murphree," 197.
17. OR 39, 3, 497-498; Van Horne, *Life of General George H. Thomas,* 266, 297.

Chapter Eight. A Reckoning

1. OR 39, 1, 699; Doolittle, "Defense of Decatur" 3:269.
2. OR 39, 1, 703; Jones, *Civil War in Decatur,* 16; Heitman, *Historical Register,* 379, 469; *History of the Seventy-third Indiana,* 208; Reid, *Ohio in the War,* 555; Spiller, *Dictionary of American Military Biography,* 1:209-212. Corbin had a distinguished career in the army after the war. He spent fourteen years in the infantry, ten of them in continuous duty at forts on the southwestern frontier, Texas, New Mexico and Arizona. Later as a brigadier general he served as adjutant general of the army. He commanded the Division of the Philippines, then was promoted to lieutenant general as commander of the Northern Division, U.S.A. He had a large part in planning during the Spanish American War. He retired in 1906 after declining the post of Chief of Staff of the army offered him by William Howard Taft, then Secretary of War.
3. OR 39, 3, 523.
4. Anderson, *Campaigning with Parson's Texas,* 148.
5. OR 45, 1, 651.
5a. Tarrant to Gale, After-Action Report.
5b. Ibid.; Williams to Gale, After-Action Report.
6. Davis, *Confederate Generals,* 1:201.
7. OR 39, 1, 702.
8. OR 39, 1, 701, Andes and McTeer, *Loyal Mountain Troopers,* 170-171.
9. OR 39, 3, 522.
10. Hood, *Advance and Retreat,* 312.
11. OR 39, 3, 913.
12. OR 52, 2, 773.
13. OR 39, 3, 879.
14. OR 39, 1, 869; Horn, *Army of Tennessee,* 383.
15. OR 39, 1, 871; Cox, "March to the Sea," 10, 16.
16. OR 52, 2, 769, 772; OR 39, 3, 868, 871.
17. OR 39, 3, 805; OR 32, 3, 805; Hay, *Hood's Tennessee Campaign,* 58; Vandiver, "General Hood as Logistician," 150.
18. Moore, "Mobility and Strategy," 113.
19. OR 39, 2, 848, 875; OR 39, 3, 888-889; Connally, *Autumn of Glory,* 481.
20. Van Horne, *Life of General Thomas,* 267; Sword, *Confederacy's Last Hurrah,* 279.

21. OR 39, 3, 499.

22. Ibid., 613.

23. Vegetius, *Military Institutions of the Romans,* 71.

24. Goff, *Conferate Supply,* 217; Henderson, *Science of War,* 639; Hood, *Advance and Retreat,* 331.

25. OR 39, 3, 470; Doolittle, "Defense of Decatur" 3:266.

26. OR 39, 2, 878; Roman, *Military Operations of General Beauregard,* 289.

27. OR 39, 3, 534; Piatt, *General George H. Thomas,* 536.

28. OR 39, 3, 483-484; Piatt, *General George H. Thomas,* 562; Van Horne, *History of the Army of the Cumberland,* 2:190, 207.

29. Cox, "March to the Sea," 2; OR 39, 3, 530.

30. OR 39, 1, 605, 607; *Personal Memoirs of General D.S. Stanley,* 191-192; Stone, "Repelling Hood's Invasion" 4:441.

31. OR 39, 1, 607, 908; OR 39, 3, 522, 540, 545.

32. OR 39, 1, 583; *Memoirs of General William T. Sherman,* 2:162; Schofield, *Forty-six Years in the Army,* 165.

33. OR 39, 1, 590; Cox, "March to the Sea," 17-18; Stone, "Battle of Franklin," 439; Van Horne, *Life of General Thomas,* 264; Piatt, General George H. Thomas, 558.

34. Cox, "March to the Sea," 4-5.

35. Piatt, *General George H. Thomas,* 559; OR 39, 2, 466.

36. OR 39, 3, 858, 883; OR 52, 2, 772.

37. OR 39, 3, 918.

38. *Memoirs of General William T. Sherman,* 2:167.

39. OR 39, 3, 904, 917; OR 39, 1, 583-584; Connally, *Autumn of Glory,* 488; Van Horne, *History of the Army of the Cumberland,* 2:185.

40. OR 39, 3, 522; Van Horne, *History of the Army of the Cumberland,* 170; Roman, *Military Operations of General Beauregard,* 2:293.

41. Sanders, "Hood's Tennessee Campaign," 290; Horn, *Tennessee's War,* 293, 294; Horn, *Army of Tennessee,* 381; McMurry, *John Bell Hood,* 165.

42. McMurry, *John Bell Hood,* 167.

43. McDonough, *Five Tragic Hours,* 15.

44. McMurry, *Two Great Rebel Armies,* 130.

45. McPherson, *Battle Cry of Freedom,* 811.

46. Henderson, *Science of War,* 643.

47. OR 45, 1, 651.

48. Horn, *Decisive Battle of Nashville,* 6-7.

49. McDonough, Five Tragic Hours, 15; McMurry, *John Bell Hood,* 159, 167, 190; Vandiver, "General Hood as Logistician," 151.

50. OR 45, 1, 660.

51. Hood, *Advance and Retreat,* 270.

51a. OR 39, 1, 699.

52. Van Horne, *History of the Army of the Cumberland,* 2:170.

53. Doolittle, "Defense of Decatur" 3:273.

54. McMurry, *John Bell Hood and the War,* 167.

Chapter Nine. Epilogue

1. Cox, "March to the Sea," 64-65; Hood, "Invasion of Tennessee," 4:432.

2. Cunningham, "Events Leading to the Battle," 18.

3. Ibid.; Cunningham, "Battle of Franklin," 101; OR 45, 1, 684-686; Livermore, *Numbers and Losses,* 131-132.

4. OR 45, 2, 639-640; Livermore, *Numbers and Losses,* 132.

4a. Joy, "The Stampede at La Fayette, GA.," 477.

5. OR 45, 2, 757; OR 45, 2, 759; OR 45, 1, 42, 46, 655, 674; Horn, *Decisive Battle of Nashville,* 420.

6. OR 45, 1, 1241, 1251.

7. OR 45, 2, 726; "Captains R.L. Cobb and F.O. Gracey," 249-252; Cunningham, *Reminiscences of the Forty-first Tennessee,* 45; Stockdale, *Death of an Army,* 151.

8. "Autobiography of Maj. D.W. Sanders," 371; Horn, *Army of Tennessee,* 420; McMurry, *Two Great Rebel Armies,* 131-132; O'Connor, *Hood: Cavalier General,* 258-259.

9. OR 45, 2, 384, 493; Fleming, *Civil War and Reconstruction,* 255; Knox, *History of Morgan County,* 187.

BIBLIOGRAPHY

Adamson, A.P. *Brief History of the Thirtieth Georgia Regiment.* Jonesboro, GA: Freedom Hall Press, Inc., 1987.

Anderson, John Q., ed. *Campaigning with Parson's Texas Cavalry Brigade, CSA: the War Journals and Letters of the Four Orr Brothers, 12th Texas Cavalry Regiment.* Hillsboro, TX: Hill Junior College, 1967.

Andes, John W. and Will A. McTeer. *Loyal Mountain Troopers: The Second and Third Tennessee Volunteer Cavalry in the Civil War.* Maryville, TN: Blount County Genealogical and Historical Society, 1992.

Auer, Louise Cheney. "Queen of the Texas Ghost Towns." *The Cattleman* 56 (May 1970) 126-128.

Bailey, Ronald H. and the Editors of Time-Life Books. *Battles for Atlanta.* Alexandria, VA: Time-Life Books, Inc., 1985.

Berlin, Ira, Joseph P. Reidy, Leslie S. Rowland, eds. *The Black Military Experience.* London: Cambridge University Press, 1982.

Berry, Chester D. *Loss of the Sultana and Reminiscences of Survivors.* Lansing, MI: published by the author, 1892.

Bevens, William E. *Reminiscences of a Private.* Fayetteville: University of Arkansas Press, 1992.

Boatner, Mark M., III. *The Civil War Dictionary.* New York: David McKay Co., Inc., 1959.

Brewer, George E. "Incidents of the Retreat from Nashville." *Confederate Veteran* 18 (July 1910) 329.

Brewer, Willis. *Alabama: Her History, Resources, War Record and Public Men.* Montgomery: W. Brewer, 1872.

Brown, Norman D., ed. *One of Cleburne's Command: the Civil War Reminiscences of Capt. Samuel T. Foster, Granbury's Texas Brigade, CSA.* Austin: University of Texas Press, 1980.

Campbell, T.H. *The Upper Tennessee.* Chattanooga: published by the author, 1932.

"Captains R.L. Cobb and F.O. Gracey." *Confederate Veteran* 3 (August 1895) 249-252.

Chadick, Mrs. W.D. "Civil War Days in Huntsville: A Diary by Mrs. W.D. Chadick." *Alabama Historical Quarterly* 9 (Summer 1947) 195-333.

Coggins, Jack. *Arms and Equipment of the Civil War.* Garden City, NY: Doubleday & Co., 1962.

Collins, John L. "Sad Story of the War." *Confederate Veteran* 6 (March 1898) 116.

Confederate States of America Papers. Fourteen Service Records
    Abstracts. Austin: University of Texas, Center for American History.
Connally, Thomas L. *Autumn of Glory*. Baton Rouge: Louisiana State
    University Press, 1971.
Cooper, James Litton. "The Civil War Diary of Captain James Litton
    Cooper, September 30, 1861 to January, 1865." *Tennessee Historical
    Quarterly* 15 (June 1956) 141-167.
Coulter, E. Merton. *The Confederate States of America, 1861-1865*. Vol. 7
    of *A History of the South*. Edited by Wendell Holmes Stephenson
    and E. Merton Coulter. Baton Rouge: Louisiana State University
    Press, 1950.
Cox, Jacob D. "The March to the Sea, Franklin and Nashville." Vol. 10
    of *Campaigns of the Civil War by Union Writers*. New York: Charles
    Scribner's Sons, 1882.
____. *The Battle of Franklin*. New York: Charles Scribner's Sons, 1897.
Crumpton, Washington Bryan. *A Book of Memories 1842-1920*.
    Montgomery, AL: Baptist Mission Board, 1921.
Cunningham, Sumner A. *Reminiscences of the Forty-First Tennessee
    Regiment*. n.p., 1872.
____. "Battle of Franklin." *Confederate Veteran* 1 (April 1893) 101-102.
____. "Events Leading to the Battle." *Confederate Veteran* 18 (January
    1910) 17-18.
Daniel, Larry J. *Cannoneers in Gray: The Field Artillery of the Army of
    Tennessee*. 1861-1865. Tuscaloosa: University of Alabama Press,
    1984.
____. *Soldiering in the Army of Tennessee*. Chapel Hill: University of
    North Carolina Press, 1991.
Darden, Pat, Capt. To Maj. A.P. Mason, After-Action Report, 1 Nov 64.
    New Orleans: Tulane University. Joseph Jones Collection.
Davis, William C. and Julie Hoffinan, eds. *The Confederate Generals*. 6
    vols. National Historical Society, 1991.
Dodson, W.C., ed. *Campaigns of Wheeler and His Cavalry 1862-1865*.
    Atlanta, GA: Hudgins Publishing Co., 1899.
Donovan, Timothy H., Roy K. Flint, Arthur V. Grant Jr., Gerold P.
    Stadler, Thomas E. Greiss, serial editors. *The American Civil War*.
    West Point, NY: U.S. Military Academy, 1987.
Doolittle, Charles C. "The Defense of Decatur, Alabama." In *Sketches of
    War History, 1861-1865: Papers of the Military Order for the Ohio
    Commandery of the Loyal Legion of the United States*. 3 vols. Edited
    by Robert Hunter. Cincinnatti: Robert Clark & Co., 1890.

Dubose, John W. *General Joseph Wheeler and the Army of Tennessee.* New York: Neale Publishing Co., 1912.

Dunnavant, Robert Jr. *Decatur, Alabama: Yankee Foothold in Dixie.* Athens, AL: Pea Ridge Press, 1995.

Dyer, John P. *The Gallant Hood.* Indianapolis, New York: The Bobbs-Merrill Co., 1950.

Eggleston, E.T. "Scenes Where General Tilghman was Killed." *Confederate Veteran* 1 (October 1863) 196.

Elliott, James W. *Transport to Disaster.* New York: Holt, Rinehart and Winston, 1962.

Fisk, John. *The Mississippi Valley in the War.* Boston and New York: Houghton, Miffiin & Co., 1902.

Fleming, Walter, L. *Civil War and Reconstruction in Alabama.* Cleveland, OH: Arthur H. Clark Company, 1911.

Foote, Shelby. *The Civil War: A Narrative.* 3 vols. New York: Random House, 1974.

French, Samuel G. *Two Wars.* Nashville, TN: The Confederate Veteran, 1901.

Gay, Mary A.H. *Life in Dixie During the War.* Atlanta, GA: Charles P. Byrd, 1897.

Gibbon, John. *The Artillerist's Manual.* Westport, CT: Greenwood Press, 1860. Reprinted 1971.

Gibbons, Tony. *Warships and Naval Battles of the Civil War.* New York: W.H. Smith Publishers, 1989.

Goff, Richard D. *Confederate Supply.* Durham: Duke University Press, 1969.

Goodloe, Albert T. *Confederate Echoes.* Washington, D.C.: Zenger Publishing Co., 1983.

Graham, E.M., Diary. John B. Long papers. Austin: University of Texas, Center for American History.

Guernsey, Alfred H. and Henry M. Alden. *Harpers Pictorial History of the Civil War.* New York, London: Random House, 1866.

Harris, A.W. Sr. to Maj. G. Storrs. After-Action Report, 2 Nov 64. New Orleans: Tulane University, Joseph Jones Collection.

Haskins, James, Capt. After-Action Report, 2 Nov 64. New Orleans: Tulane University, Joseph Jones Collection.

Hay, Thomas Robson. *Hood's Tennessee Campaign.* New York; Walter Neale, 1929.

Heitman, Francis B. *Historical Register and Dictionary of the United States Army.* Washington, D.C.: Government Printing Office, 1903.

Henderson, George F.R. *The Science of War: A Collection of Essays and Lectures*. Edited by Capt. Neill Malcom. London: Longmans, Green & Co., 1908.

Henderson, Lillian. *Roster of Confederate Soldiers of Georgia*. 6 vols. State of Georgia, Confederate Pension and Records Dept., 1960.

High, Edwin C. *History of the 68th Indiana Volunteer Infantry*. Matamora, IN: 68th Indiana Infantry Association, 1902.

History of the Seventy-third Indiana Volunteers in the War of 1861-65. Seventy-third Indiana Regimental Association. Washington, D.C.: The Carnahan Press, 1909.

Hood, John B. *Advance and Retreat: Personal Experiences in the United States and Confederate Armies*. Secaucus, NJ: Blue and Grey Press, 1985.

____. "The Invasion of Tennessee." In *Battles and Leaders of the Civil War*. 4 vols. Edited by Robert V. Johnson and Clarence C. Buel. New York: Thomas Yoseloff, 1887-1888.

Horn, Stanley, F. *The Decisive Battle of Nashville*. Baton Rouge: Louisiana State University Press, 1956.

____. *The Army of Tennessee*. Wilmington, NC: The Broadfoot Publishing Co., 1987.

____. ed. *Tennessee's War 1861-1865*. Nashville: Tennessee Civil War Centennial Commission, 1965.

Indiana, Adjutant General. *Report of the Adjutant General of Indiana*. 8 vols. Indianapolis: 1866.

Jenkins, William H. and John Knox. *The Story of Decatur, Alabama*. Decatur: Mayor and City Council of Decatur, 1970.

Jones, Joseph. "Roster of the Medical Officers of the Army of Tennessee." *Southern Historical Society Papers* 22 (1894) 165-280.

Jones, Mary Miles, ed. *The Gentle Rebel: The Civil War Letters of 1st. Lt. William Harvey Berryhill, Co. D, 43d Regiment, Mississippi Volunteers*. Yazoo City, MS: Sassafrass Press, 1982.

Jones, Maurice J., *The Civil War in and Around Decatur, Alabama*. Typescript. In possession of the author, Decatur, AL.

Joy, Charles Gore. "The Stampede at La Fayette, Ga." *Confederate Veteran* 20 (October 1912) 473-477.

Knox, John. *A History of Morgan County, Alabama*. Decatur, AL: Morgan County Board of Revenue, 1967.

Kolb, R.F., Capt. To Adj., After-Action Report, 2 Nov 64. New Orleans: Tulane University. Joseph Jones Collection.

Last Roll. *Confederate Veteran* 13 (September 1905) 424.

Last Roll. *Confederate Veteran* 22 (June 1910) 280.

Lavender, John W. *They Never Came Back: The War Memories of Captain John W. Lavender, CSA.* Edited by Ted R. Worley. Pine Bluff, AR: W.M. Hackett & D.R. Perdue, 1956.

Lee, Stephen D. "Lieutenant General S.D. Lee's Report of the Tennessee Campaign, Beginning September 29th, 1864." *Southern Historical Society Papers* 3 (1877) 64-67.

"Lieutenant General Schofield." *Confederate Veteran* 3 (September 1895) 274.

Lindsley, John Berrien. *Military Annals of Tennessee.* Reprint. Spartanburg, SC: The Reprint Co., 1974.

Livermore, Thomas L. *Numbers and Losses in the Civil War in America 1861-65.* Boston and New York: Houghton, Mifllin & Co., 1900.

Lonn, Ella. *Desertion During the Civil War.* New York, London: The Century Co., 1928.

Lossen, Christopher. *Tennessee's Forgotten Warriors: Frank Cheatham and His Confederate Division.* Knoxville: The University of Tennessee Press. 1989.

Lyon, Mrs. Adelia C., comp. *Reminiscences of the Civil War.* San Jose, CA: William P. Lyon Jr., publisher, 1907.

Mahon, John F. "Civil War Infantry Tactics." In *Military Analysis of the Civil War, An Anthology* by the Editors of "Military Affairs." Millwood, NY: KTO Press, 1977.

Maxwell, James R. *Autobiography of James Robert Maxwell of Tuscaloosa, Alabama.* New York: Greenberg, Publisher, 1926.

McDonough, James L. and Thomas L. Connally. *Five Tragic Hours.* Knoxville: The University of Tennessee Press, 1983.

McMurry, Richard M. "Rise to Glory: A Speculative Essay on the Early Career of John Bell Hood." In *Rank and File,* edited by James T. Robertson, Jr. and Richard McMurry. San Rafael, CA: Presidio Press, 1976.

_____. *John Bell Hood and the War for Southern Independence.* Lexington: The University Press of Kentucky, 1982.

_____. *Two Great Rebel Armies.* Chapel Hill: University of North Carolina Press, 1989.

McPherson, James M. *Battle Cry of Freedom.* Oxford: Oxford University Press, 1988.

McTeer, Will A. *Autobiography of Major Will A. McTeer 1843-1925.* Edited by Marion R. Mangrum. Maryville, TN: Maryville Enterprise, 1967.

McWhiney, Grady. *Southerners and Other Americans.* New York: Basic Books, Inc., 1973.

Mercur, James. *Attack of Fortified Places.* New York: John Wiley & Sons, 1914.

Miller, Rex. *The Forgotten Regiment.* Williamsville, NY: The Patrex Press, 1984.

Miller, J.M. *Recollections of a Pine Knott in the Lost Cause.* Greenwood, MS: Commonwealth Publishing Co., 1900.

Mitchell, Enoch D., ed. "Letters of a Confederate Surgeon in the Army of Tennessee to his Wife." *Tennessee Historical Quarterly* 5 (June 1946) 172-177.

Moore, John G. "Mobility and Strategy in the Civil War." In *Military Analysis of the Civil War, An Anthology* by the Editors of "Military Affairs." Millwood, NY: KTO Press, 1977.

Morgan, Thomas J. "Reminiscences of Service with Colored Troops in the Army of the Cumberland, 1863-65." In *Rhode Island Narratives of the Rebellion,* Series 3, No. 13. Providence: Soldiers and Sailors Historical Society of Rhode Island, 1885.

Nelson, H.K. "Tennessee, a Grave or a Free Home." *Confederate Veteran* 15 (November 1907) 508.

Nevin, David. *The Civil War: Sherman's March.* Alexandria, VA: Time-Life Books, Inc., 1986.

Noyes, Edward, ed. "Excerpts from the Civil War Diary of E.T. Eggleston." *Tennessee Historical Quarterly* 16 (December 1958) 336-358.

O'Connor, Richard. *Hood: Cavalier General.* New York: Prentice-Hall, Inc., 1949.

Ohio General Assembly. *Official Roster of the Soldiers of the State of Ohio in the War of the Rebellion, 1861-1866.* 12 vols. Cincinnatti, Ohio Valley Press, 1888.

Palfrey, John C. "General Sherman's Plans After the Fall of Atlanta." In *Papers of the Military Historical Society of Massachusetts.* 8 vols. Edited by Theodore F. Dwight. Wilmington, NC: Broadfoot Publishing Co., 1910.

Piatt, Donn and Henry V. Boynton. *General George H. Thomas, A Critical Biography.* Cincinnatti: Robert Clark & Co., 1893.

Plum, William R. *The Military Telegraph During the Civil War in the United States.* Chicago: Jansen, McClurg & Co., 1882.

Reid, Whitelaw. *Ohio in the War: Her Statesmen, Her Generals and Soldiers.* 2 vols. Cincinnati: Moore, Wilstack & Baldwin, 1868.

Rennolds, Edwin H. *History of the Henry County Commands Which Served in the Confederate States Army.* Jacksonville, FL: Sun Publishing Co., 1904.

Ripley, Warren. *Artillery and Ammunition of the Civil War.* New York: Promontory Press, 1970.

Ritter, William L. "The Disastrous Expedition to Sherman's Rear." *Southern Historical Society Papers* 11 (1883) 537-539.

Robertson, John, ed. *Michigan in the War.* Lansing, MI: State of Michigan, 1882.

Roman, Alfred. *Military Operations of General Beauregard.* 2 vols. New York: Harper & Brothers, 1884.

Romeyn, Henry. "With Colored Troops in the Army of the Cumberland." In *War Papers: Being Papers Read Before the Commandery of the District of Columbia, Military Order of the Loyal Legion of the United States.* Wilmington, NC: Broadfoot Publishing Co., 1903.

Rountree, Benjamin. "Letters from a Confederate Soldier." *Georgia Review* 18 (Fall 1964) 267-297.

Rowland, Dunbar. *Military History of Mississippi.* Spartanburg, SC: The Reprint Co., 1988.

Sanders, David Ward. "Autobiography of Maj. D.W. Sanders." *Confederate Veteran* 18 (August 1910) 370-372.

____. "Hood's Tennessee Campaign." *Southern Bivouac* 3 (November 1884) 97-104; (December 1884) 145-153; (January 1885) 193-302; (February 1885) 242-252; (March 1885) 289-294; (April 1885) 350-366.

Schmutz, George S. *History of the 102d Regiment Ohio Volunteer Infantry.* Wooster, OH: G.S. Schmutz Co., 1907.

Schofield, John M. *Forty-six Years in the Army.* New York: Century Co., 1897.

Sherman, William T. *Memoirs of General William T. Sherman.* 2 vols. Bloomington, IN: Indiana University Press, 1957.

Shannon, Issac N. "Sharpshooters with Hood's Army." *Confederate Veteran* 15 (March 1907) 123-126.

Smith, Daniel P. *Company F, First Alabama Regiment.* Rev. ed. Gaithersburg, MD: Butternut Press, 1984.

Spiller, Roger J., ed. *Dictionary of American Military Biography.* 3 vols. Westport, CT: Greenwood Press, 1984.

Stanley, David S. *Personal Memoirs of Major General D.S. Stanley, USA.* Cambridge, MA: Harvard University Press, 1917.

Steryx, H.E., ed. "Autobiography and Civil War Letters of Joel Murphree of Troy, Ala." *Alabama Historical Quarterly* 19 (Spring 1957) 170-208.

Stockdale, Paul H. *The Death of an Army: The Battle of Franklin and Hood's Retreat.* Murfreesboro, TN: Southern Heritage Press, 1992.

Stone, Henry. "Repelling Hood's Invasion of Tennessee." In *Battles and Leaders of the Civil War.* 4 vols. Edited by Robert V. Johnson and Clarence C. Buel. New York: Thomas Yoseloff, 1956. Reprint.

_____. "The Battle of Franklin, Tennessee, November 30, 1864." In *Papers of the Military Historical Society of Massachusetts.* 8 vols. Edited by Theodore F. Dwight. Wilmington, SC: Broadfoot Publishing Co., 1989.

Sword, Wiley. *The Confederacy's Last Hurrah.* Lawrence, KS: University Press of Kansas, 1993.

Sykes, Columbus. Papers. Kennesaw Mountain National Battlefield Park, National Park Service, Marietta, GA.

Tarrant, Edward, Capt. to Capt. W. Gale, 2 Nov 64. New Orleans: Tulane University. Joseph Jones Collection.

Taylor, F. Jay, ed. *Reluctant Rebel: The Secret Diary of Robert Patrick, 1861-1865.* Baton Rouge, LA: Louisiana State University Press, 1959.

Tennessee, Adjutant General. *Report of the Adjutant General of the State of Tennessee of the Military Forces of the State from 1861 to 1866.* Nashville: S.C. Mercer, Printer to the State, 1866.

Thomas, Wilbur. *General George H. Thomas, the Indomitable Warrior.* New York: Exposition Press, 1964.

Thompson, William Y. *E.M. Graham North Louisianan.* Lafayette: Center for Louisiana Studies, University of Southwestern Louisiana, 1984.

Tower, E. Lockwood, ed. *A Carolinian Goes to War. The Civil War Narrative of Arthur Middleton Manigault.* Columbia: University of South Carolina Press, 1983.

U.S. Government Printing Office. *The War of the Rebellion: A Compilation of the Official Records of the Union and Confederate Armies, 1861-1865.* 128 vols. Washington D.C.: 1880-1891. Referred to in notes as OR.

_____. *Official Records of the Union and Confederate Navies in the War of the Rebellion.* 31 vols. Washington, D.C.: 1894-1922. Referred to in notes as ONR.

U.S. Navy, Naval History Division. *Civil War Naval Chronology, 1861-1865.* Washington, D.C.: 1971.

Vandiver, Frank E. *Ploughshares into Swords: Josiah Gogas and Confederate Ordnance.* Austin: University of Texas Press, 1952.

_____. "General Hood as Logistician." In *Military Analysis of the Civil War, an Anthology* by the Editors of "Military Affairs." Millwood, NY: KTO Press, 1977.

Van Horne, Thomas B. *History of the Army of the Cumberland.* 2 vols. Cincinnatti. OH: Robert Clark & Co., 1875.

———. *The Life of Major General George H. Thomas.* New York: Charles Scribner's Sons, 1882.

Vegetius, Flavius Renatus. *The Military Institutions of the Romans.* Edited by Thomas R. Phillipps. Harrisburg, PA: The Stackpole Co., 1960.

Warner, Ezra J. *Generals in Gray.* Baton Rouge: Louisiana State University Press, 1959.

———. *Generals in Blue.* Baton Rouge: Louisiana State University Press, 1964.

Wheeler, Joseph. *Alabama.* Vol. 8 of *Confederate Military History Extended Edition.* Edited by Clement A. Evans. Wilmington, NC: Broadfoot Publishing Company, 1987.

Whiteside, Myrtle F. "The Life of Lawrence Sullivan Ross." Masters thesis, University of Texas, 1938.

Williams, George W. *History of the Negro Troops in the War of the Rebellion.* New York: Bergman Publishers, 1968.

Williams, Samuel C., Lt. Col. to Capt. Gale. After-Action Report, 3 Nov 64. New Orleans: Tulane University, Joseph Jones Collection.

Wilson, Suzanne Colton. *Column South with the Fifteenth Pennsylvania Cavalry.* Flagstaff, AZ: J.F. Colton & Co., 1960.

Wisconsin, Adjutant General. *Annual Report of the Adjutant General of the State of Wisconsin for 1865.* Madison: William J. Park, 1866.

Wolseley, Garnet Joseph. "An English View of the Civil War." *The North American Review* 149 (December 1889) 713-727.

Womack, Bob. *Call Forth the Mighty Men.* Bessemer, AL: Colonial Press, 1987.

Woodworth, Steven E. *Jefferson Davis and His Generals. The Failure of Confederate Command in the West.* Lawrence: University Press of Kansas, 1990.

Worsham, W.J. *The Old Nineteenth Tennessee Regiment, CSA.* Knoxville, TN: published by the author, 1902.

Wright, Marcus J. *Texas in the War, 1861-1865.* Edited by Harold B. Simpson. Hillsboro, TX: Hill Junior College Press, 1965.

Yeary, Mamie. *Reminiscences of the Boys in Gray, 1861-1865.* Dayton, OH: Morningside House, 1986.

Zorn, William A. *Hold at All Hazards.* Greenville, SC: published by the author, 1987.

INDEX

Adams, 2nd Lt. Elias, 99
Adams, Brig. Gen. John, 54-55, 106, 128, 158
Alabama and Tennessee River Railroad, 14
Alatoona, Georgia, 17, 18, 45
Andrews, Col. Julius A., 45
Anniston, Alabama, 6
Apthorpe, lst Lt. George W., 107
Armstrong, Brig. Gen. Frank C., 25, 159
Athens, Alabama, 3, 12, 15, 32, 39, 60, 75, 140, 142-143
Atkinson, Lt. Col., 122
Atlanta, Georgia, 2, 4-8, 10-11, 25-26, 30, 32, 36, 45, 76, 142-147
Atlanta-Chattanooga Railroad, 17

Bainbridge, Alabama, 118-120, 126, 154-155
Baker, Capt. C.W., 107
Barger, Lt. H.C., 47
Bate, Maj. Gen. William B., 93, 98, 158
Beach, Capt. Albert F., 38, 48-49, 51-52, 65, 74, 101, 103, 113, 133
Beard's Bluff, Alabama, 37
Beauregard, Gen. P.G.T., 8-9, 12, 23-25, 30-33, 61, 63, 71-72, 118-120, 131,
        135, 137, 139-141, 145-148
Bennettsville, Alabama, 29
Berry, Lt. Oscar L., 98
Berryhill, Lt. W.H., 55, 68, 116
Bevens, Cpl. William E., 56, 123
Big Shanty, Georgia, 4, 17
Blake, Capt. Edgar W., 38, 47
Bledsoe, Capt. Hiram M., 160
Blountsville, Alabama, 30, 34-37
Blue Creek Church, Alabama, 35
Blue Mountain, Alabama, 6, 10, 14, 19, 117
Boyles, Col. William, 159
Bragg, Gen. Braxton, 15, 137, 141
Brewster, Lt. G.H., 61
Bridgeport, Alabama, 15-16, 21, 23-25, 28, 32, 34, 38, 67, 135, 144-146,
        150, 162
Broady, Sgt. Andrew C., 50
Brooks, Pvt. Mark, 52
Brooksville, Alabama, 29, 35
Brooner, Pvt. George, 115
Brown, J.H., 52

Brown, Maj. Gen. John C., 34, 41, 69-71, 112, 142, 157
Brown's Ferry, 142, 163
Bryant, Pvt. John A., 50
Bullock, Capt., 47
Bullock, Col. Robert, 158
Butler, Pvt. Thomas J., 45
Byrd, Pvt. James L., 45

Cahaba, Alabama, 39
Carroll, Pvt. Patrick, 49
Carter, Brig. Gen. John C., 157
Castle Morgan, prison camp, 39
Caswell, Maj. Theodore D., 93
Cave Springs, Georgia, 30, 124
Cedar Bluff, Alabama, 28
Cedartown, Georgia, 17
Chadick, Mrs. W.D., 17, 61, 117
Chattanooga, Tennessee, 2, 4, 7, 11, 23, 32, 34, 67, 75, 117, 129, 141-144
Cheatham, Maj. Gen. Benjamin F., 18, 28-29, 32, 34-35, 41, 45, 58, 64, 66, 69,
     71, **80**, 112, 123-124, 152, 157, 159
Cherokee, Alabama, 137-138, 146
Chickamauga, 5, Rock of, 10
Claysville, Alabama, 37
Clifton, Tennessee, 24, 118
Cobb, Maj. Robert, 160
Cobb, Capt. Robert L., 155
Cockrell, Brig. Gen. Francis M., 18, 110, 158
Colbert County, Alabama, 42
Collins, Sgt. Jesse, 11
Columbia, Tennessee, 152, 155
Columbus, Mississippi, 20, 26
Cooper, Capt. Charles S., 38, 48, 51
Coosa River, Georgia, 32
Corbin, Lt. Col. Henry C., 67, 74, **89**, 101, 103, 105, 109, 117, 130
Corinth, Mississippi, 14, 23-24, 31, 118, 120, 137, 145, 148
Cornelia, Alabama 29-30
Corse, Gen., 18
Courtland, Alabama, 19, 32, 36, 72, 118, 119, 123-124, 126, 137, 142,
     146-147
Cowan, Capt. J.J., 42, 53, 102, 113-114, 160
Cox, Brig. Gen. Jacob D., 144
Cox, Pvt. William, 45
Cross Roads, Georgia, 21
Croxton, Brig. Gen. John T., 16, 126, 141

Crumpton, Pvt. Washington B., 68
Cumberland, Army of the, 3, 10, 12, 67
Cunningham, Col. Sumner A., 112-113, 124, 155

Dalton, Georgia, 4, 10, 12, 18, 23, 30, 67, 143
Danville, Alabama, 128
Darden, Capt. Pat, 42, 44, 52, 70, 100, 103, 109, 114, 132, 160
Davis, Lt. B.K., 52
Davis, President Jefferson, 4-5, 8-9, 135, 139, 141, 151
Day's Gap, Alabama, 128
Decatur, Alabama, 1-3, 11-13, 15-17, 19-20, 25, 30, 32-39, 41-45, 53, 58-60,
      62-64, 66-68, 70-72, 75-76, 98-99, 110-111, 113-114, 116-117, 119-120,
      124-130, 134-143, 145-146, 148-152, 154-156, 163
Decatur, Georgia, 5, 111
Dodge, Brig. Gen. Grenville M., 2-3
Doolittle, Col. Charles C., 12-13, 38, 44, 46-48, 50-53, 103, 109, 121, 125,
      130, 133, 150
Drake, Elisha Steele, 109
Duck River, Tennessee, 155

Eaton, Capt. William C., 60
Ector, Brig. Gen. Matthew D., 45, 158
Eddy, Lt. Col. E. Frank, 50
Elzey, Maj. Gen. Arnold, 17, 159
Espy, Lt. Col. Harvey J., 75, 109
Ewing, Maj. E.W., 138

Featherston, Brig. Gen. Winfield S., 100, 106, 132, 158
Flewellen, Pvt. Robert, 66, 125
Florence, Alabama, 11, 25, 75, 126, 139, 147, 149, 154, 163
Forrest, Lt. Moreau, 17
Forrest, Maj. Gen. Nathan B., 8, 10, 11, 14-15, 24, 27, 30-31, 33, 39, 61, 67,
      111, 118, 134-135, 140, 142-143, 149, 152, 154
Fort Deposit, Alabama, 37
Fort No. 1, 13, 46, 48, 52, 93-96, 121
Fort No. 2, 13, 47-48, 51, 60, 94-96, 121
Foster, Capt. Samuel T., 26, 112
Franklin, Tennessee, 2, 26, 54, 68, 70, 99, 112, 148, 152-153
French, Maj. Gen. Samuel G., 18, 27, 35, 44-45, 62, 71, **82**, 110, 123, 147,
      155, 158

Gadsden, Alabama, 1, 10, 19, 23-24, 26-27, 29-30, 32, 34, 37, 61-62, 71, 117-
      118, 124, 134-135, 145, 147-149
Gallatin, Tennessee, 67

Garth, Gen. Jesse Winston, 42, 71-72, 118
Gay, Mary A.H., 111
Gaylesville, Alabama, 1, 27-28, 33-34, 75-76, 117, 120, 135, 143
General Burnside, General Grant, General Sherman (gunboats), 17, **79**
General Thomas (gunboat), 16, 37, 113, 114, 117, 124
Gentry, Sgt. J.W., 45
Gill, Mrs., 19
Gillette, Lt. Frank, 114
Gist, Brig. Gen. States Rights, 69, 157
Given, Col. William, 38, 47, 60, 130
Golding, Jo, 68
Golightly, Pvt. David, 98
Goodloe, 1st Lt. Albert T., 42
Gordon, Brig. Gen. George W., 36, 157
Graham, Capt. Evander M., 36-37, 123
Granger, Brig. Gen. Robert S., 1, 12-17, 19, 37-38, 53, 60-61, 65-67, 72-76, **78**,
     93-95, 97-98, 103, 105, 107-108, 110, 113-115, 119-120, 122, 126-127,
     130, 131, 134, 140, 142-143, 149, 155
Granbury, Brig. Gen. Hiram B., 111, 157
Grant, Gen. Ulysses S., 2-4, 6, 14, 19, 28, 62, 76, 143-144
Green, Col. Peter V., 157
Green Lake, Texas, 99
Gunter's Ferry, Alabama, 62
Guntersville, Alabama, 1, 15, 21, 23-24, 29-31, 33, 37-38, 71, 134, 136, 149

Hall, Col. Jairus W., 110, 126
Halleck, Maj. Gen. Henry W., 19, 76, 119, 129, 139
Hardee, Lt. Gen. William J., 5, 29
Harlan, Marion, 54
Haskins, Capt. James, 42, 52, 70, 100, 109-110, 160
Hightower, Capt. Raleigh, 99
Hinds-McEntire home, 95, 156
Hobson's Island, Alabama, 113
Hodges, Pvt. John E., 98
Hood, Lt. Gen. John B., 1-2, 5-10, 12-35, 37-38, 41-42, 46-47, 52-53, 61-63,
     66, 71-72, 75-76, **77**, 93, 98, 110, 115-123, 126-127, 130-142, 144-155,
     157
Horn, Stanley F., 147
Houghton, Col. Moses B., 99
House, George, 47
Howard, Maj. Gen. Oliver O., 61-62
Hulburd, Maj. Edwin M., 38, 111
Huntsville, Alabama, 12, 17-18, 32, 37-38, 53-54, 60, 110-111, 113, 117-118,
     121, 129, 145, 163

Indianola, Texas, 99, 111

Jackson, Tennessee, 24, 118
Jackson, Brig. Gen. William H., 24-25, 29-30, 54, 124, 135, 159, 160
Jacksonville, Alabama, 17, 22-23, 25, 31, 120, 137
"Jeff Davis," (Gen. Hood's horse), 5
Johnson, Cpl. "Tommie," 53
Johnsonville, Tennessee, 136, 143
Johnston, Gen. Albert Sidney, 45
Johnston, Gen. Joseph E., 4-5, 10, 18, 37, 54, 155
Jones, Col. John S., 110
Joy, Charles Gore, 154

King, Sgt. Samuel, 108
Kriedler, Lt. John C., 65

Lamb's Ferry, Alabama, 120
Lavender, Capt. John W., 57
Lee, Gen. Robert E., 3-4, 22
Lee, Lt. Gen. Stephen D., 7, 18, 28-29, 34-35, 41, 61, 98, 126, 152, 159
Lee, Wesley, 40
Lewis, Brig. Gen. Joseph H., 159
Limestone County, Alabama, 43
Little River, Alabama, 27, 62
Loring, Maj. Gen. William W., 35, 41, 44, 47, 50, 54-55, 70-71, **83**, 107, 110, 116, 123, 128, 132, 158
Lovejoy's Station, Georgia, 6
Lowrey, Brig. Gen. Mark P., 157
Lucas, Pvt. Francis, 99
Lyon, Col. William P., 17, 37, 53, 113

Maddock, Sgt. John, 121
Manigault, Brig. Gen. Arthur M., 7
Marietta, Georgia, 23, 68
Maryville, Tennessee, 50
Maxwell, Sgt. James R., 124
McCartney Hotel, 104
McDaniel's Mill, 41
McDermid, Cpl. Angus, 59
McFall, Sgt. James, 96
McMicken, Col. M.B., 7
McReynolds, Capt. Aaron G., 50
McTeer, Lt. Will, 45, 49, 65, 95-96, 104, 108, 125
Meade, Maj. Gen. George G., 3

Memphis, Tennessee, 28, 39-40, 51
Memphis and Charleston Railroad, 3, 12, 23, 31, 38, 123, 137, 141
Miller, Pvt. J.M., 55
Mills, Joseph E., 128
Mitchell, Col. William D., 98, 158
Mize, Sgt. Rufus L., 50
Mobile, Alabama, 4, 6, 117, 127, 155
Mobile and Ohio Railroad, 23, 31, 137, 139
Moore, Capt. William C., 94-95, 97, 132
Mooresville, Alabama, 32
Morgan, Col. Thomas J., 67, 73-74, **88**, 101-109, 121-122
Morton, Master Gilbert, 16, 113
Moulton, Alabama, 19, 34, 66
Murfreesboro, Tennessee, 22, 99, 110, 129
Murfreesville, Alabama, 30
Murphree, Sgt. Joel D., **87**, 128
Muscle Shoals, Alabama, 28, 63
Myrick, Maj. John D., 42, 160

Nashville, Tennessee, 1-3, 7, 10-11, 14, 21-22, 24, 46, 53, 57, 59-61, 75, 99,
    110, 116, 118-119, 136, 139-40, 142-144, 146-148, 153-155
Nashville-Chattanooga Railroad, 2, 25, 21, 147
Nations, Pvt. Reuben, **90**, 116
Naylor, Capt. W.A., 16, 103
Nelms, 2nd Lt. M.B.F., 98
Neuse, Pt. R.L., 73
Newberry, Pvt. James, 49

Oakville, Alabama, 66
Oakville, Texas 112
Ohio, Army of the, 3
"Old Straight," 29
Oleander, Alabama, 30, 36
Olmstead, Col. Charles H., 157
O'Neal, Col. Edward A., 159
Orr, A.L., 131
Osburn, Lt. Norval, 38
Ovenden, Pvt. Sampson, 111
Owen, Dr. Urban G., 59
Oxford, Alabama, 32, 145
Ozanne, Lt. John M., 70

Palmetto, Georgia, 6-8, 10, 138, 141, 149
Patrick, Robert, 35

Pettus, William D., 54
Pilcher, Maj. Mat, 70
Polk, Lt. Gen. Leonidas, 29
Polk Home, 156
Pontoon bridge (at Decatur), 3, 34, 52, 60, 65, 73, **92**, 100, 132-133, 150, 154
Porter, Col. George C., 157
Prosser, Lt. Col. W.F., 38, 47-50, 65, **84**, 96
Pulaski, Tennessee, 15, 67, 75, 140, 142-143, 152

Quarles, Maj. Gen. William R., 55-56, 68, 159

Reaves, Pvt. Andrew, 50, 73
Red Hill, Alabama, 29
Redwine, Capt. J.O., 99
Reed, Capt. Myron W., 47, 96
Resaca, Georgia, 4, 18
Reynolds, Brig. Gen. Daniel H., 56, 159
Reynolds, Lt. E.H., 112
Robertson, Pvt. James J., 50
Roddey, Brig. Gen. Phillip D., 8, 15, 19, 24, 30-31, 38, 44, 46-47, 66, 118, 154
Rolph, Capt. A.H., 107
Rome, Georgia, 18, 32, 100, 120, 129, 143-144, 146
Romeyn, Capt. Henry, 100-102, 105, 108, 109
Rosecrans, Maj. Gen. William S., 11, 119
Ross, Brig. Gen. Lawrence S., 25, 124, 159
Rousseau, Maj. Gen. Lovell H., 15

Sanders, Maj. D.W., 62, 146
Sansom, Emma, 27
Saylor, Col. Thomas, 46, 50
Schofield, Maj. Gen. John M., 129, 143, 152-153
Scott, Brig. Gen. Thomas M., 41, 44-45, 58, 106, 116, 122, 128, 158
Scruggs, Mr., 41-42
Sears, Brig. Gen. Claudius W., 158
Selma, Alabama, 14, 20, 23, 26-27, 30, 32, 39, 110, 118, 139, 145
Shannon, Pvt. Isaac W., 70
Shelbyville, Alabama, 124
Sherman, Roger, 55
Sherman, Maj. Gen. William T., 1-11, 14-15, 18-19, 21-25, 27-28, 33-34, 37, 55, 62, 72, 75-76, 117-120, 128, 134-135, 138-148, 150
Shoup, Brig. Gen. Francis A., 42
Smiddy, Pvt. James, 73
Smith, Maj. Gen. A.J., 11, 119
Smith, 2nd Lt. Daniel P., 55, 59, 68, **91**

Smith, Brig. Gen. James A., 160
Smith, Gen. Kirby, 153
Smith, Col. Melancton, 159
Smith, Brig. Gen. Thomas B., 158
Snake Creek Gap, 22
Snooks, Lt., 43-45
Somerville, Alabama, 19, 35, 37-38, 41, 66, 72, 102
Souers, Dr. John A., 97
Spence, S.A., 52
Spring Hill, Tennessee, 152
Stanley, Maj. Gen. David S., 28, 62, 141-143
Steedman, Maj. Gen. James B., 115, 134, 141, 155
Stephens, Pvt. Charles H., 98
Stewart, Lt. Gen. Alexander P., 17-18, 27, 29-30, 34-35, 41-42, 46, 55, 58, 70-71, **81**, 99, 123-124, 127, 132-133, 152, 158, 160
Stevenson, Alabama, 1, 3, 12, 15, 21-23, 32, 34, 37-38, 67, 72, 75-76, 119, 129, 134-137, 139, 140-141, 144-148
Stevenson, Brig. Gen. John D., 3
Stokes, Pvt. Thomas J., 111-112
Stone, Pvt. John F., 51
Stone River (gunboat), 16, 38, 46-47, 60, 66, 103, 107, 113-114
Storrs, Maj. George S., 160
Strahl, Brig. Gen. Otho F., 112, 157
Streight, Col. Abel D., 27
Sultana (steamer), 39, 51
Swoope, Mr., 123
Sykes, Lt. Col. Columbus, 54, 68
Sykes, Capt. Edward T., 54
Sykes, Adjutant William E., 54-55, 67

Tarrant, Capt. Edward C., 42, 44, 52, **86**, 100, 109, 114, 132, 160
Taylor, Lt. Gen. Richard, 8, 15, 23, 30-32, 61, 118, 136-137, 155
Taylorville, Alabama, 52
Tennessee Campaign, 1, 9, 21-22, 27, 68, 118, 147-149
Tennessee River, 1, 11, 14, 21, 28, 31, 71, 132, 150, 154
Thomas, Maj. Gen. George H., 1-2, 10-16, 19, 21-22, 28, 37-38, 53, 62-63, 65-67, 72, 75, 98, 110, 119-120, 122, 126, 128-129, 134, 139, 140-144, 147, 152-154
Thompson, 5th Sgt. James M., 99
Thornburgh, Lt. Col. Jacob M., 65, 74, 95-97, 111
Tobin, Lt. James, 74
Triana, Alabama, 43, 163
Trotter, Asst. Surgeon T. R., 128
Trueheart, Maj. Daniel, 42, 124, 160

Tullahoma, Tennessee, 143
Tupelo, Mississippi, 155
Turner, Capt. William B., 159
Tuscaloosa, Alabama, 124
Tuscumbia, Alabama, 14-15, 19, 22-24, 26, 30-31, 59, 66, 118-119, 120-121,
    128, 135-140, 145-147, 149, 152, 163

Vaughan, Brig. Gen. Alfred J., 34, 36
Vail, Maj. Nicholas J., 101-103, 105, 115

Wade, Lt. Col. Alfred B., 75, 96, 103
Walthal, Maj. Gen. Edward C., 35, 42, 44, 55-56, 68-69, 123, 127, 154, 159
Walthal, Capt. Felix L., 99
Waties, Capt. John, 160
Warrenton, Alabama, 29, 37
Watkins, Mr., 123
West Point, Georgia, 26
Wheeler, Maj. Gen. Joseph, 22-23, 24-25, 30, 32, 34, 37, 61-62, 67, 75, 117,
    120, 135, 142, 145-146, 159
White, Capt. Giles E., 75, 97
Whitesburg, Alabama, 113
Whiteside, Miss Maggie, 124
Wilkinson, Pvt. Cary H., 116
Wilkinson, Craig Hamilton, 55
Williams, Lt. Col. Samuel C., 42, 99-100, 132, 160
Williamson, Maj. Thomas G., 38, 48, 50
Wilson, Lt. Alexander, 66
Wilson, Capt. James C., 66, 130
Windes, Lt. Col. F.M., 154
Winstead Hill, Tennessee, 152
Wolseley, Lord, 1
Woodworth, Lt. Charles, 121-122
Worsham, W.J., 69

Young, Brig. Gen. William H., 45, 158

Praise for

The

LOST PAPERS

of Confederate General John Bell Hood

Stephen M. Hood

Author of John Bell Hood: *The Rise, Fall, and Resurrection of a Confederate General*

"By locating, editing, and publishing *The Lost Papers of Confederate General John Bell Hood,* Sam Hood has made an immense contribution to the history of the Civil War. General Hood may be perhaps the most misunderstood of the eight full generals of the Confederacy, and these vastly important documents fill in many of the blanks in the historical record. No Civil War collection will be complete without this book."

— Winston Groom, author of *Forrest Gump and Shrouds of Glory: From Atlanta to Nashville: The Last Great Campaign of the Civil War*

"New Civil War era papers are found each day, but none will have the impact of General Hood's private papers. We now know what was important to Hood, what he was working on, his relationships with political and military notables, and who he was as a citizen, husband, and father. Detailed medical reports for his Gettysburg and Chickamauga wounds reveal much about his physical condition—the subject of endless speculation—and letters from prominent Confederate officers shed fresh light on the dramatic events in Tennessee in late 1864. Given the major revelations in these papers, Hood's memoir, *Advance and Retreat,* deserves a new look. What a great Sesquicentennial gift to the history of the American Civil War!"

— Len Riedel, Executive Director, Blue and Gray Education Society

"Few personalities in the Civil War are more intriguing and captivating than John Bell Hood, yet he remains clouded by characterizations made of him by historians who were convinced there was no documentary proof to question what they wrote. That has changed! These newly found documents by and about John Bell Hood provide an entirely new picture of the gallant general and his relationships with other Confederate commanders and his wife Anna. Here also are the remarkable reports of Hood's very capable surgeon, John T. Darby, describing in intricate detail his Gettysburg and Chickamauga wounds, the operations, the recuperations, and the effects of all of that upon Hood, all written by the one person most qualified to so testify. Finally we see the real John Bell Hood, and he is a wonder to behold!"

— Kent Masterson Brown, author of *Retreat From Gettysburg: Lee, Logistics and the Pennsylvania Campaign,* and *Meade at Gettysburg: A Study in Command*

Praise for

JOHN BELL HOOD

The Rise, Fall, and Resurrection of a Confederate General

STEPHEN M. HOOD

Winner of the Albert Castel and Walt Whitman book awards

"A deftly written and ably presented work of impressive and seminal research."
— *Midwest Book Review*

"John Bell Hood was one of few Confederate generals who held important commands in both Virginia and the Confederate West. Given command of the defense of Atlanta, Hood fought to hold the city but failed. He later led the army in the unsuccessful Tennessee Campaign, where he was unable to cut off Schofield's Union army at Spring Hill, was bloodily repulsed the next day at Franklin, and routed two weeks later at Nashville. Historians and writers since then have denied Hood his day in court, thus shaping a very negative opinion of the general. But Sam Hood's scholarship in John Bell Hood has shown that contemporary views of Hood were often much different from the perpetuated stereotypes. His study demonstrates anew the complexity of history and the importance of impartiality by those who write it."

— Brandon H. Beck, Professor Emeritus, McCormick Civil War Institute, Shenandoah University

"The time is right for Sam Hood's book. Another way of looking at it is, my, what we have learned since the Civil War's Centennial fifty years ago."

— Stephen Davis, award-winning author of *Texas Brigadier to the Fall of Atlanta: John Bell Hood* and *Into Tennessee and Failure: John Bell Hood*

"The Civil War historical community can only benefit from Sam Hood's dedication and perseverance in presenting a full . . . review and strong defense of JBH's life and service. Readers will certainly understand the general better."

— *Journal of America's Military Past*

"Highly recommended."

— *Midwest Book Review*

ABOUT THE AUTHOR

Noel Carpenter and wife Betty, 1955

A native son of Decatur, Alabama, Noel Carpenter (1918-2000) was born to English immigrants and grew up with his older sister in the family home on Line Street, now preserved in the Old Decatur Historic District. As a boy he played on the sites where General Hood's Army of Tennessee had engaged Union forces in 1864.

After graduating from the University of Alabama and earning his M.B.A. from the University of North Carolina, he spent 30 years as a command pilot and chief of data automation in the U.S. Air Force, attaining the rank of Lt. Col. His military service was followed by a second career in data processing at the Texas Department of Health in Austin.

Retirement gave him the opportunity to combine a lifelong interest in Civil War history with his military perspective to examine in depth the action that had taken place in his hometown. He spent twelve years researching and writing his account.